Jessie Benton Frémont

**The story of the guard:**

A chronicle of the war - Vol. 2

Jessie Benton Frémont

**The story of the guard:**
*A chronicle of the war - Vol. 2*

ISBN/EAN: 9783337730956

Printed in Europe, USA, Canada, Australia, Japan

Cover: Foto ©ninafisch / pixelio.de

More available books at **www.hansebooks.com**

# THE STORY OF THE GUARD:

## A CHRONICLE OF THE WAR.

### By JESSIE BENTON FRÉMONT.

"Their good swords rust,
And their steeds are dust,
But their souls are with the saints, we trust."

BOSTON:
TICKNOR AND FIELDS.
1863.

Entered according to Act of Congress, in the year 1864, by
TICKNOR AND FIELDS,
in the Clerk's Office of the District Court for the District of Massachusetts.

RIVERSIDE, CAMBRIDGE:
STEREOTYPED AND PRINTED BY H. O. HOUGHTON.

"That the honorable enterprises, noble adventures, and deeds of arms, performed in the wars between England and France may be properly related, and held in perpetual remembrance — to the end that brave men taking example from them may be encouraged in their well-doing, I sit down to record a history deserving great praise; but, before I begin, I request of the Saviour of the world, who from nothing created all things, that He will have the goodness to inspire me with sense and sound understanding, to persevere in such manner, that all those who shall read may derive pleasure and instruction from my work, and that I may fall into their good graces.

"It is said, and with truth, that all towns are built with many different stones, and that all large rivers are formed from many springs; so are sciences compiled by many learned persons, and what one is ignorant of is known to another; not but that everything is known sooner or later." . . . . — *Sir John Froissart's Preface to his Chronicles of England, France, &c.*

WHEN this book was written, nearly a year ago now, it was my wish and hope to be able through it to get some immediate assistance for the families upon whom the winter was coming without their usual support. It was to have been issued as a Christmas Story, at the kindly season when "good-will towards all" would be propitious to my attempt. But various causes delayed it. Among others the want of a publisher who was willing to incur the risk of publishing what might be taken as a disapproval of an official act. Mr. Ticknor and Mr. Fields hearing of it, volunteered for the service, but it was already too late for a Christmas-book and so it was put off to a more favorable season. When a new command was given to the General we hoped for renewed service for the Guard, and this stayed my hand again. Again disappointed for them, I have no restraining motive, but launch it now, taking shame to myself for deferring for any cause a right act. For in this, as well as in great matters, I do not believe that there is any specially appointed "more convenient season."

19th October, 1862.                                    J. B. F.

# PREFACE.

---

"THE REASON WHY."

[*From a Letter to Mr. Fields.*]

. . . . . . . .

BECAUSE I know what it is I mean to do, I am afraid I fell into the error of talking to you this morning as though you, too, knew all about it. Mr. Ticknor and yourself talked "book," when I am incapable of writing a book; sunshine puts out little fires, and I've known too much of those who lived, as well as wrote books, to pale my ineffectual fires by comparison. But I can tell what I know. I believe that those truly soldierly young men, worthy of a place in chronicles of knightly deeds, were misrepresented, slighted, and finally insulted out of the service, because of the name they bore. This has not altered the feeling with which they took that name, and we feel to them as toward the foremost in sharing a hard siege. It seems to me as much an obligation of feeling and honor to do them justice, and heal the hurts to their just pride, as it would be to visit them in the hospital, had they been wounded bodily in the discharge of their duty near the General in the field.

They were all young, many with younger members of their families looking to them for protection and assistance; some few were married; some were sons of widows;—and it was an additional sorrow to find that those killed at Springfield comprised the greater number of married men and some of the most needed sons.

I cannot let those mothers and wives feel our name only the synonyme of sorrow and loss to them. In the first nights after hearing of Springfield (the days were too busy for dwelling on thoughts) this thought troubled me. The idea of making the noble conduct of the Guard the means of providing for their families then came to me like an inspiration. It leaves no sense of obligation, and their protection from such of the ills of life as money affects will be due to the same true hearts and strong hands that defended the country at Springfield. Mr. Raymond was at the piano while I was thinking this over, and chanced upon one of his German student songs, which so fitted to and embodied the Charge, that we adopted it at once as the Song of the Guard; and then and there, in the midnight hours, we made each our contribution to this Story of the Guard. I had the General's letters, telling me very fully of the Charge and many incidents connected with it. Major Corwine, who was Judge Advocate on the staff, had the deepest interest in the "Kentucky Company," which he had mainly recruited himself; and the Song is from the memories of Capts. Howard and Raymond, who made the English translation, and arranged it for the piano. The Song is, I think, perfectly charming: — opening with measured, muffled, tramping minor chords, it breaks into the open key to be gathered at the close of each verse into one quivering minor chord on the word "Dying."

Here where the war is unseen, and comparatively unfelt, it is hard to make real the feeling with which Union people hold to each other in a rebel State actually at war. In St. Louis, the rebel city of a rebel State, where until September the uniform of a Federal officer made him at once a target, those who shared the chances of that earlier day of insecurity were as one household. Disturbances in the city were of almost nightly occurrence. The house used as Headquarters was strongly built and fire-proof, and part of the basement was a regular armory, from which ammunition was issued more than once "in the small hours" to the Guard, for some dangerous duty in the city and its suburbs. We literally, and the city figuratively, slept over a magazine. Those were wearing days and anxious nights, but the city learned to rest in peace, trusting to the watchfulness of the Provost Marshal General McKinstry, and to Colonel McNeill. Few knew of the constant activity and perpetual vigilance of Zagonyi and the Guard. Many of these young men were citizens of St. Louis, and knew the sources of danger. As the work of the department became centralized, and telegraphic and other government records were to be taken care of at Headquarters, the Guard was put on duty inside of the house, where many hundred persons were daily passing to and from the various offices.

It is smooth sailing in St. Louis now; but the first company of the Guards are among those who remember a different order of things.

This is to you a digression; but I mean it to explain why we had for the Guard a more personal feeling than could grow up in ordinary war or in the formal life of barracks.

. . . . . . . .

I will put together such material as I have, and leave it to you to make it successful. You will see it is impossible to make a regular "book" of it, — it is really nothing more than the fireside story of the Guard; interesting from the facts, — interesting because in ten thousand homes some vacant place will lend a stronger interest to the tale. I hope something, too, from the kindly interest of old friends of my father's.

These young men gave their lives to save the State he loved so well and served so long. Some rest there, as he does, until the last trumpet-call.

For any personal object I should never use my name which has been to me a double charge to keep, but I think my father also would more than approve, when it is to do justice and to aid the widow and the orphan.

Such as it is, my offering goes to make a fund for them, and I turn over the manuscript to you, relying on your experience and good sympathy to manage the rest. My part is to give you the story of the Guard, and yours is to make it profitable to them. If Mr. Ticknor and yourself will be bankers, the Rev. Mr. Eliot, in St. Louis, and Major Corwine, in Cincinnati, will see a just use made of the fund. The Newhall family would look up any Philadelphians of the Guard, — for there may be some needs from tedious wounds, and a wounded soldier is as worthy of care as even children and women. But with this I have nothing to do. My part is to collect and arrange some facts and incidents, and give them with all my best wishes for success to the tribunal I was educated to believe in — a faith confirmed by my own experience.

JESSIE BENTON FRÉMONT.

NEW YORK, 5th December, 1861.

# THE STORY OF THE GUARD.

## I.

THERE was a time — not long ago if measured by months — when so quiet and remote was the life we led that I found out then who read the whole of magazines, and new books, and even newspapers; and through this bond of a past experience have learned to realize that somewhere facts are taken in and cherished, make roots, and bear fruit. Our brain-rations came twice a month, and, although a month old when they did reach us, had about them a freshness and zest which had never been obtained in long city experience. How faithfully everything gets read, and how living and real the creations of fancy get to be in this healthy slowness of absorption. This is talking mysteries to the regular citizen who has never known a long interval — a good wearing interval — of a year or two years of genuine country life, which (when it's over) it's worth having gone through for the new perceptions acquired. A mental Græfenberg process to one accustomed to turn only to the few preferred pages of some favorite author, and throw by the rest of the magazine. Where but in countriest country does one hear, " I won't cut the leaves yet — I've not finished the last number "? Where else does the dreadful certainty obtain that there is time and to spare for *both numbers!* But when the solitude and fasting from print begin to tell, and give the natural flavor to simples, then comes a real enjoyment of reading such as book-stores *à discretion* cannot yield.

You are in some green solitude where there is no collection of books within many miles, — in a new State perhaps, — and you see it is going to rain again, or snow, and you have read up everything. "You" means a woman, of course; a man would be glad of a long rain, or a snow and a thaw, that would give him some quiet days for going over papers in-doors; but you have no papers, and all your days are quiet, and if it rains, you "can't get out." You have no letters to answer, if you've been "in the country" a year; — the term of mourning is over for you, long ago, and the long letters of the first months have subsided into rare, —

"I have been trying to find time to

write you a long letter, but we've been so busy with this, that, and the other, and are you *never* coming back?"
and such like polite vaguenesses, so that you feel you are, to all intents and purposes, ghosts on a foreign shore.

It is mail-day, (you have become blunted to the fact that there are intermediate days which are not mail-days,) and you watch, and even listen for the horse's feet. For your genuine country mail comes only within an easy ride of your house, and you connect by coachman and horse with mail-coach. There he comes! You don't see the parcel. It's a small mail, then, and carried in the pocket. You rather hang back from knowing your fate, but it comes to you, if you won't meet it, and says, remorselessly, — "Stage couldn't cross Dry Creek." That's the way of Dry Creeks — not to turn a mill-wheel in pleasant weather, and suddenly to grow into a roaring torrent in the course of a night. You ask in sarcastic tones, that would make Naiads wretched, if they were acquaintances, " When will Dry Creek be fordable?" and get for answer, " Well, if it rains, (and 'pears like rain, — if it don't rain by night, it's most sure to rain before daylight,) why then you'll allow they won't git over before next week — four or five days, anyhow." You know the man to be fearfully experienced in weather-signs, and yield to the impassable gulf of a Dry Creek modified by the rainy season.

Of course it rains; and the horrid papers that bar you out from companionship are taken up, and silence sets in. So you devote yourself to toning-down to indoor-pitch two boys whose riotous health rather endangers the needed quiet; and when at last they're off to bed, with a compliment for their good behavior, (carrying off your honors!) you feel your mind is fagged and longing for the rest of fresh ideas. Being a woman, you want to read, in place of going wholesomely to sleep at early candle-light. Then it is that the lesser stars find their chance to shine. You pile on more wood, draw the lights nearer, and gathering all the last mail, go through it again. Rare, and always to be treasured, are the exceptional times when in this deep, secure solitude and stillness some book that was indeed a book rose on the night, and took its place among the things that are joys forever. On such a night as this, I read the "Idylls of the King." Not a human sound to break the stillness —

the hum from the great fire of logs, the scraping of the oak boughs against the roof — the straining, rushing sound of the wind among the pines, and that undefinable mourning wail made by coming storms among mountains — to this accompaniment I read of rude Geraint, and too-patient Enid, with her brave song — of Elaine and her sweetest story of true girlish love, and the half disgust that might well come over Lancelot as he realized " what might have been "— of the impossible Arthur, humanized by his woful wrongs, and brought within our sympathies by his grand courtesy and forbearance — then re-reading of that closing scene where the good knight, having fought his last fight, and lying so deeply smitten through the helm, had yet one drop more of bitter held to his lips. Sir

Bedivere had the grace to repent and feel ashamed, but first he gave his king and friend one more turn of the screw — it belongs with Peter's weeping. The wind drawing through the narrow valley between the high mountain ranges made a weird but noble harmony with the wail that rose from the funeral barge.

But all this digression is only to show that out of those years of seclusion I brought away new perceptions, and now that I am back among books, having, as Bridget Elia says of prints, "nothing to do but to walk into Colnaghi's" and get my fill, I often remember that past time; and, because I know many more read in that way than in the unsatisfactory surface manner one must in cities, I will venture to hope for this little story a thorough reading, with a kindly appreciation of the many feelings that make its telling not intrusive, I trust.

The wire-net tables at the florists, with their showy exhibition of stemless flowers, bear the same relation to the garden-beds, where their mates are yet blooming and growing, as the ordinary city reader does to those who have leisure to feel, and to whom I commend this Christmas-tale of a great deed — told in two lines in the papers — but bringing heavy sorrow for life to some, and, to all who truly love and honor our flag, unending pride in the Body Guard.

And if any one should say, What, that old story! I beg to answer that what *De Musset* says of Love is equally true of Truth: "It is never old and never new, because it is eternal."

There is an English picture, familiar

to us through its lithographed form, called " The Telegraph."

It is the interior of a quiet English home, where mother and children are at their steady, calm, home occupations. Through the open window, over fair miles of field and wood, is seen a distant train. It concerns them not. It is rushing to a busy life that is not theirs. Their life is told by the room — in their simple occupations — in the portrait on the wall — they are to labor and to wait; he serves.

The little maid shows in the boy from the Station with a telegraphic despatch, and instantly, in the twinkling of an eye, there is a great change. Struck by lightning as effectually as though her black garments were the charred remains from that stroke, the mother is widowed, the children orphaned, by the slip of paper in her relaxed, fainting hand.

When in the telegraphic news-column we read,

"Major Zagonyi, with one hundred and fifty of the Body Guard, attacked and drove from Springfield over two thousand rebels, with a loss of only fifteen men,"

some women knew that that "fifteen" carried a death-stroke to as many hearts. Prayers that this cup might pass from her went up with fear and trembling from many a wife and mother. Some days must pass before the fearful doubt settles into a worse fact. Give your tenderest pity to the mother who learned in the same day that at Little Gauley and at Springfield two boys, her sons, — and she was a widow, — lay dead.

## II.

#### WHY THE GUARD WAS FORMED.

In addition to the usual reasons for cavalry, the prairie nature of the country to be operated over, and the habits of its settlers, made a special need for efficient cavalry in the army of the Mississippi. In this abundant grain region, where the most negligent farming is amply remedied by the natural prairie growth of forage, riding-horses are as much a matter of course as work-horses only would be on a Northern farm. The rifle hangs over every fireplace; between game and Indians, it has little rest. Given a gun and a horse, the inevitable result on the frontiers is a hunter; if a war comes, the cavalry soldier is ready. Opposing infantry would be laughed to scorn by these men, to whom horsemanship, the country to be gone over, and a brave enemy, are equally familiar.

In Missouri, this war material acquired something of a military organization from the protracted struggles with Kansas, and was fostered and protected by government money and ammunition, and the powerful aid of government favor. For four years preceding the war, government patronage and political honors were the portion of the faithful to the Southern side; and the same agency made it unprofitable and unpopular and, in the city of St. Louis, unfashionable, to be with the North and for Freedom.

It was necessary to form our brave and willing but comparatively untrained men into cavalry, which could not only compete with the frontiersmen and their tough horses in the things they knew, but, having other knowledge added, be their superiors in any encounter. A shameful number of regular officers had deserted; those who remained were nearly all on duty east of the Mississippi Valley; and the difficulty of officering and rendering efficient the masses of untrained troops was a serious embarrassment.

Fortunately our adopted citizens recognized that Freedom was of no nationality; and the swords that had been used in its behalf in Germany and Hungary were taken down and offered to aid in saving its very hearth-stone, as the United States had seemed to them.

Among those of whose tried skill and courage many incidents had been told to us, there was one whose particular qualities and experience pointed him out as best qualified to form and elevate to the highest standard a body of young men who were to be chosen with the purpose of forming a school for cavalry officers, from which, as regiments were raised, instructed officers could be taken: and which could be at the same time the nucleus for a regiment itself. The long residence of many Hungarian officers in our midst has brought home to us many incidents of their brave struggle; and one, among others, related of Zagonyi showed him to have not only the coolness and experience that was needed, but that rarer quality, the capacity for generous and unselfish devotion. He proved this in twice saving the life of General Bem at the utmost danger to his own, — the last time ending in Bem's escape and his own wounding and long imprisonment.

When I asked Zagonyi the particulars of the day at Hermanstadt, his surprise was great to find we knew of it at all; only with much persistence could I get even confirmation from him. His additions to the story were remembrances of others, — of an aid to General Lüders (Russian), who stopped a soldier from firing upon him as he lay wounded and pinned down by his dead horse, and how he had had him carried off and cared for as his condition required; of the old bugler who would stay by him defending him until he forced him to go on and save the General, (Bem) — and so on. These experiences, grafted on a thorough military education, made Zagonyi the fittest one to carry out the cavalry plan; and I will give his own account of the forming of the Guard, in his own quaint Hungarian English, which gives it more emphasis and character, and makes a brief, soldierly effect which is not natural to pens feminine.

I once heard a good criticism made unconsciously by that natural knight and gentleman, our friend Kit Carson.* In preparing a sketch of his life, a writer used the expression, "there he snared the wily beaver." Carson came to me about it. He did not like to hurt the writer's pride; but said he, "there's men that will read that, and they'll know every word of that had to come from me or them, and it's not true that I *snared* beaver. Beaver must be caught with *traps*." So I got it unsnared, and comforted him; and, profiting by Carson's criticism, I let the actors

* Colonel Carson, now on active duty in New Mexico.

speak for themselves. I should explain that all that I give from Major Zagonyi was taken down, at one sitting, roughly, as memoranda, not as a smooth, connected account, — for which there was not time.

## III.

(ZAGONYI SPEAKING.)

"At the outbreak of the rebellion I had the idea to recruit cavalry, but the order appeared that only one regiment will be accepted from all the loyal States; this at once cooled down all the zeal what I had, being unable to understand how, without cavalry, will carry on the war, — knowing by experience that in no country, and less in America, (so big it is,) can any general accomplish this with success. Cavalry is necessary for the security of an army; without that, no reconnoitring can be made on the enemy's ground, — incursions so in small as large scale to annoy them day and night, disturbing them so that they shall never have a night's repose, beside covering our own movements so completely that the enemy shall not be able to form any exact idea from what point, and by what strength, and with what disposition, and when, he shall be attacked.

"Artillery is to fight the battle. Cavalry is to find where to fight it, and how to finish it.

"Was the intention now to form a body of picked men, each to be as officer. As was raised regiments, could be taken from this corps well-trained officers.

"Commenced on the tenth August. On twelfth, was sworn in first company, and was excluded over two hundred men. Besides, from seven States came application by letters. These, and inside pressure in St. Louis, compelled the General to order a second company. After came the offer of the Kentucky company, which, Kentucky being in such a "—— (motion of the hand like a boat rocking) " the General could not refuse. Having three companies, through the cavalry regulation, we had to raise a fourth to make the battalion. More so, because letters was lying over from lawyers, doctors, young men of good families with recommendation from governors, judges, mayors of cities, &c. Besides some from Visconsin, where I was asked that, if the General sends me with his name that he wants it, and as an officer that we know, you can have five thousand men.

"And it turned out that the fourth company beat the others, so fine it was. The fourth company was a beautiful company; was not needed to force it to be filled up.

But only hundred days' campaign cut them short that they was not to see actual service. Application was made of officers to get position in the Guard; every one was refused, being the rule that every officer was to be raised from the ranks."

(The Kentucky company elected their officers. The others Major Zagonyi selected. They were regularly mustered in for three years or the war, by an experienced mustering officer of the regular army, — Captain, now Colonel Tracy.)

"For one month I [Zagonyi] commanded the four companies, drilled them, with hardly any officers or non-commissioned officers, as captain; later, on the nineteenth September, being promoted to be a major — the regulation gives a lieutenant-colonel to four companies. Was only one captain in the four companies, Captain Foley, by election; the rest of the officers was as lieutenant, and was every one fit to be captains and even major, one, and he never served before. They was put through hard drilling, riding in the school, besides going out every day on the outskirt of the city and made through all the manœuvres that in the field can be used, and it did cost many a bruised face and body and a couple of ribs. So that they had hardly any time for rest or amusement. Besides, in the midnight received orders many a time to march out in fifteen twenty minutes, to be on the ground where intended disturbances was expected, to be ready for every emergency—and generally was fifty men ordered, and before the fifty left the camp every man who had horse and saddle was in the rank,—nobody would remain behind. I selected every horse; not a single horse came in the Guard which did not go through my inspection.

"The evening before we left St. Louis we did not have sabres enough, nor did the rest of the cavalry regiments. I found out, (Capt. Callender was perfectly rough and used me badly; I had to tell him, Excuse me, Captain, but I never took an insulting word, and you must answer me decently,) in short, I find out from a trusted man that sabres was at the arsenal before Capt. Callender knew it, and the order was written and gone to the arsenal before he knew they are there.

"Sabres, Beale's revolvers, and Colt's carbine with stock attachment, which we disattached in the attack, using revolver only.

Besides, the night before leaving camp by Jefferson City, the General gave each officer a pair of revolvers. Was well armed and well mounted."

## IV.

### THEIR DEPARTURE.

Unprepared as other things were, the right season had come; and many points were right which marked this as the time for an advance of the army, first against the rebel force under General Price, and—after freeing the State from that and establishing peace in the rear—then to commence the downward move to New Orleans. This ultimate object was comprehended by the whole army, to whom, as Western men, the Mississippi was the natural tide to fortune, for want of whose commerce their States were perishing. It was with the quick coöperation of interest as well as patriotism that they entered into the idea of making every sacrifice for success. Very willingly, therefore, they took the field, only partially equipped in clothing, and very partially in provisions. One single track railway, and a river with more snags and sandbars than water, at that season, were the only means of getting the large army and its supplies up to Lexington, which was the point moved against, about two hundred and fifty miles above St. Louis. The river was unusually low, and the weather remained sunny and open. A small gunboat, improvised from a ferry-boat,\* and carrying five nine-inch Dahlgren guns, was relied on for river-service, and much was hoped from her aid at Lexington. But no

---

\* Since famous under Captain Porter as The Essex. She was then The New Era, and commanded by Captain Rodgers, who had superintended her fitting out.

ingenuity could get her to draw less than five and a half feet, and on some of the bars there was not four feet water.

When the retreat of Price turned the movement more immediately southward, it seemed as if difficulties would vanish. Corn was getting ripe and hard in the fields, cattle could be secured by scouts and driven on the hoof, fresh corn-meal could be had wherever there were mills, and a day's halt could always be made to grind enough; or, if that delay would lose valuable time, they could, for the object, live on meat alone. All along their route the forage would be in the right state in the fields, so that the delays and expense of great transportation trains were to be avoided, and yet neither men nor animals suffer. With Memphis and New Orleans in the near future, hardships were felt to be temporary.

Time enough for feasting or fastidiousness when the victory was won.

It was a stirring, eager, hopeful time, that just before their leaving St. Louis. The offices and halls at headquarters were humming with life, and the clank and ring of sabre and spur were sounding-notes of coming battle all the day long, and far into the nights.

More harmonious and efficient coöperation could not be than that received by the General from his staff: — there were also some loyal citizens whose brief visits always resulted in advantage to the army. Working so late into the nights, it got to be one of our habits to have tea Russian-fashion, — so that without keeping the servants from their rest, we could still have it to refresh us and keep us roused. It will always stay with me as one of the most pleasant memories of that most wearing and most welcome work of my life, how they came to that cool upper-hall, and in a hurried interval drank tea, and gave condensed summaries of the work or news; —sometimes several would gather at the same time, and little animated discussions would go on, the latter part of the time chiefly as to what could be done without. It was so good to see the kind smile of amusement with which the veterans in exposure listened to such arguments. Such sufferings outlined in a few words, as would sometimes come from them! It made a respectful blush cover the young faces that had been planning what they thought sacrifices. "Is no need of tents," says General Asboth. "In Hungary we make a winter campaign and we sleep without tents, our feet to the fire,—sometimes our ears did freeze," (the General's ears and his feet are a long way apart). But the least concern on all minds was the open enemy in the field.

On the 26th September, they left St. Louis, — the General and a few officers going by rail, and the Guard with their horses by the somewhat slower route of the river. Really, necessary stores and transportation were wanting; and it must be borne in mind, that, but for these impediments General Price would have been certainly overtaken, his army most probably defeated, and quiet for the winter secured to Missouri. The New Year would have found our flag at Memphis, and, it was reasonably hoped, the usual spring trade would descend the river to New Orleans.

To accustom the troops to feel their

strength was part of their training, and occasions for skirmishing were always accepted. The oldest troops in this Mississippi army were hardly of the date at which Bonaparte was willing to use his, — six weeks; but the longest drill could not have made them more patient of hardship, more self-denying, or more cheerful under fatigue and privation. "New Orleans, and home again by summer," was their mainspring. Sigel earned the name of the "Flying Dutchman," so jealously did he keep his division in the advance, — General Asboth nearest him, — General Frémont, with the Guard, overtaking Sigel and keeping up with him.

In this good heart they started. The following letters belong here.

"JEFFERSON CITY, September 28, 1861.

" MADAME, —

" I am now on *waiting duty* in the hall, and Jack is busily engaged in writing despatches in the General's room, which contains also three beds, three tables, two wash-stands, the General himself, Colonel Eaton, one or two of the amateur aids, and a wood-fire. In short, it is 'Hd. Qrs., W. D.' condensed into a space of twelve feet square. Under these circumstances, and knowing that no one else who would think of such a thing will have the time to carry the plan into execution, Adlatus R. seizes a stray piece of paper to jot down a few of the incidents of our journey and our reception.

" We had a very quiet, slow, pleasant passage, with no other interruption than stopping at all the bridges, &c. . . .

"On reaching the depot here, we were met by Gen. Price and a red lantern, — which constituted the extent of our reception. You ought to hear Major Zagonyi hold forth on that affair. Gen. P., in citizen's clothes, bearing his lantern, led the way over mud-puddles and pitfalls, with Gen. F. and Gen. A. The unhappy staff straggled on behind. At length we arrived at the Virginia Hotel, and found that no preparations had been made for our comfort. Major White and your humble servant, the 'Adl.,' were employed till nearly twelve o'clock, in quartering the staff. If we had not studied the science of 'Quarterstaff,' I don't think we should ever have got through. Major Z., Jack and I slept in the General's office after he went to bed.

"Gen. Price — who is one of the most

good-natured men it has been my lot to meet — took Zagonyi and men to a hotel, and mildly asked, 'Can you accommodate my good friends here?' 'wich they sed they couldn't Mum.' Whereupon the gallant little major stepped up and said, 'You must give my boys to sleep, else I put you in the street,' which ended in their taking seventy-two men!

"'Every man has his Price,' you know; would that every soldier had his 'Zagonyi!'

"The mail is closing, and these little bits of intelligence are good for nothing, unless I send them soon.

"Hoping that some weary moment, beguiled by the little history of our ludicrous reception, may excuse the liberty I have taken,

"I remain, &c., &c., R."

"JEFFERSON CITY,
"29th Sept. — 8 in morning.

"YESTERDAY occupied in work of requisitions, moving ahead troops, and placing them. We feel severely the want of equipments and arms, especially for cavalry. We have, almost literally speaking, no appropriately-armed cavalry in the field. But I am hoping daily now to hear of the arrival of sabres. . . I am about going into camp this forenoon, and it threatens rain.

"Tell Dr. Van Buren that I have written for the surgeon he recommended to me, and ask him to aid to have him come.*

"See the Sanitary Committee, and tell them that the whole Surgical Department

---

* Dr. Suckley. The General had the benefit of Dr. Suckley's services in Virginia last summer.

here is in a very bad condition, — it gives me great anxiety. Therefore, as soon as they can spare Dr. Mills for a short time, I would be very glad to have him, that I may get the condition of the army in this respect better, before they get into the field. In the event of an action, we should be in a very bad condition."

"J. C. F."

## V.

### AT JEFFERSON CITY.

SEEING he should be detained some days in that place, the General telegraphed us to come up. The ride up was full of painful contrasts to my old memories and more especially my last journey through the State. I had so often gone to the frontier with Mr. Frémont, when he was starting on his overland journeys, or to meet him on his return, that my own associations with the State were of the hospitality and kind sympathy so often and so warmly given to me by its people. They would have done as much for any of my father's daughters; but to me new kindnesses were added because of

Mr. Frémont's sharing that life so full of traditions and perils. The Indian country, with its vague mountain boundary, is to frontiersmen what the sea and its dangers are to coast people—bringing like sympathies.

After seeing Mr. Frémont off in the fall of '53, I found the river so low that I left the boat which had brought me from Independence, and got off at Washington to go down by land.

Although but about eighty miles above St. Louis, the river falls so low in the autumn, that it was very probable (as proved the fact) that the steamboat would require several days to make the distance.

I was quite alone. My good Marie, tired by the rapid journey from Washington, which we were so soon to retrace, had been left in St. Louis to recruit, and so

I was landed from a little boat, without explanation or introduction, all by myself, among a whole crowd on the bank, who had gathered — it was Sunday afternoon — to watch the boat stop, and wonder at the passenger leaving it. There was no mark on my trunk, and it was rather embarrassing. The clerk of the boat had told me there were only Germans there, and no communication with the railway, which was then finished only to a point about twenty-seven miles lower down. But I was restless, and anywhere in Missouri I felt at home.

I spoke to a fatherly-looking man, to whom I explained that the river was low, and I was anxious to get to St. Louis immediately, and asked to be shown the way to the hotel. In a very grave and silent way he turned up the bank, signing me to follow, which I did, a little troubled, but much more amused by the whole crowd following in solemn silence. If it had been an American town, all the necessary, and some unnecessary, questions would have been asked and answered in the first five minutes. But we made our way up the hill and into the clean, ugly, comfortable town, and I was shown into the "best room" of a large house, whose mistress and daughters came forward and made me as quietly welcome as though they knew me. Their faces, the furniture, the violins and guitar, and high pile of music-books; the pretty bright light hair of the women, too-tightly-plaited, all were Germany itself. I pleased myself by accepting this unquestioning hospitality as it was given, and still did not give my name,

—only asking a room, as I found I could not get any conveyance until the next day. Even then, they could only offer to see about one, having nothing themselves.

It was all so odd, so primitive, so truly good and hospitable, that I was at once and most pleasantly relieved of all embarrassment. The daughters went up to prepare a room, and the mother soon showed me to it. I had taken off my hat and gloves, and was smoothing my hair, when the mother — who had remained in the room — caught up my glove, and bursting into tears, cried out a sobbing speech to me: — "Ah, dear God! You are a lady from my country; — you are from Hesse Cassel. The ladies in my country wear these gloves when they go hunting with the king. They have stopped in their carriages at my door, and I have carried them to drink. It is twenty-four years since I come away from my country; but I love it best — ah!" — and then she let the tears downfall, for the lost home.

Straight from Hesse Cassel to Missouri! — in 1829, too, when it was *so* new. She had never left her new home. Sometimes her husband went to St. Louis. Otto wanted to go there, and he was twenty-three now; he ought to go to see it, &c., &c. It was hard to make her realize I was American. "But you have color in your face!" — biennial ague was her experience, and she could not conceive of exemption from it. But when I told her who I was, I think she was as pleased as if I had been a lady hunting with the king. It loosened the tongues of all the family. My father was personally known to some, and they all held him as their own property. As they explained to me, "He is our Senator, and a friend to the Germans." One son-in-law was gone on a trading excursion towards New Mexico. His young wife attached herself to my side, and there was an unspoken bond between us. It happened to be the anniversary of the old people's wedding. They were so glad I was there that day. Such an elaborate, bountiful repast!

After the early supper, they all gathered in the large room, which was positively elegant from its glistening cleanliness, and the window-seats filled with plants, and the large table in the centre, covered with music and instruments. With the same delightful simplicity and absence of consciousness which had marked everything else among them, each took his instrument and place by the table, — sons and sons-in-law, — the father and several of the younger women taking their music, and then followed piece after piece of such music as only Germans can play rightly, — occasionally all joining in a lovely song.

Wonderfully large tumblers of beer stood by each musician, but there was but little break to what was, evidently, their habitual evening's occupation — not even when one substantial citizen after another came in to make his respects to my father through me, and to wish a good voyage to Mr. Frémont.

Very early the next morning I started to make the intervening twenty-seven miles, in the best conveyance the sudden demand could afford — a country-cart without springs, and a plough-horse. And so, in the gray dawn, I left these kind people, loaded with presents from their best vintages for my father, and followed by their kindest good wishes for myself. Otto, farmer, tenor, and guitarist, had at length his chance. He drove me to the depot, and then saw me to St. Louis, where my dear friend and cousin — whose charming home was then as now mine also, when there — made him welcome to hospitality as genuine as his own, although so different in its fashion.

I had been long revolving many memories when we reached the dining-station of Hermann — also a German town, and very near this town of Washington. Now, as then, the Germans were friends; but along the whole route guards were stationed. We moved slowly, at best, as we had a heavy train, nearly a regiment, and some artillery; and at every bridge the train stopped and parleyed with the force on guard; then, feeling the way cautiously, we moved forward again. The new timbers in some of the bridges, with the charred remains on the shore, explained some of this caution;—but everywhere the stamp of insecurity was on the country. No more careless travel among a friendly people. My good old frontier friends, I fear, are mostly gone secessionward.

It was so good to reach home-faces at the close of the day. The General was at the depot to meet us, as were quite a number of officers, whose wives had taken this last chance of seeing them. We had room for some in the large ambulance waiting for us, and drove out to the camp, while our fellow-passengers — the regiment — took the drier and more direct road over the hills, their flag seeming to wave us an assurance of welcome and protection.

Soon we were in a loyal atmosphere, where a Sibley tent, with a board floor, and a glowing camp-fire in front, made again the old pleasant effect of frontier hospitality.

Our stay was over in a few days. Early on Monday we saw the tents struck and the whole force move off; as my youngest boy said, "packed up for the battle-field," and then took our way back to St. Louis. But the day before having been very hot, the General fixed the hour before sundown for the Evening-Service, and then was the real leave-taking of the troops, who were with the rising of the sun to turn their faces away from their river and march inland. Nearest the Staff stood the Guard drawn up in open square. They justified all Zagonyi has said of them. All of nearly the same age and height, with great similarity of habits and of education, and all guided by the same enthusiasm in a noble cause, they looked what they were: the true, knightly embodiment of war. Their compact unadorned uniform of dark blue gave depth of tone to the picture, as they stood relieved against the setting sun and the nearer groundwork of autumnal foliage. At the close of the services, their band played the dear old hymn of "Old Hundred," and these manly young voices sang its grand and simple prayer, and then all heads bared to the benediction. After a moment's pause, at the regular military drum-beat they fell back to their soldier-life and walk, and went on their way, and I saw them all no more.

As the light died from the sky the camp-fires brightened on the far hill-sides; from all the camps we could hear late into the night hymn-tunes; — and so, with reverent hearts and heightened purpose, they made their farewell to their homes.

When the Emperor — then still President — gave back the Imperial Eagles to the French army, the banners were all blessed at an altar erected on the Champ de Mars. Over sixty thousand troops were on the ground, and the surrounding crowd was in hundreds of thousands. That used to stay on my memory as the grandest of religious war cérémonies: that great host bowing reverently as the sacred symbol was elevated over the emblem of the old glories of France. But far more touching and impressive is it now to remember this home-scene with all its terrible inner history of a Cain-and-Abel strife, and recognize that our army not only felt it could ask the blessing of God, but that it did so; — and it will be given. What is sown in tears and weakness now shall yet be raised in power.

---

"When I thought that a war would arise in defence
    of the right,
That an iron tyranny now should bend or cease,
The glory of manhood stand on his ancient height,
    Nor the nation's one sole God be the millionnaire;—
. . . . . . . .
And as months ran on and rumor of battle grew,
    It is time, it is time, O passionate heart, said I,
(For I cleaved to a cause that I felt to be pure and
    true,)

And I stood on a giant deck and mixed my breath
  With a loyal people shouting a battle-cry,
  Till I saw the dreary phantom arise and fly
Far into the North, and battle, and seas of death.

Let it go or stay, so I wake to the higher aims
  Of a land that has lost for a little her lust of gold,
And love of a peace that was full of wrongs and shames:
  Horrible, hateful, monstrous, not to be told;
  And hail once more to the banner of battle unrolled.

Let it flame or fade, and the war roll down like a wind,
  We have proved we have hearts in a cause, we are noble still,
And myself have awaked, as it seems, to the better mind;
  It is better to fight for the good than to rail at the ill;
I have felt with my native land, I am one with my kind,
I embrace the purpose of God, and the doom assigned."

## VI.

### EN ROUTE.

I HAVE chosen to give some letters in my possession rather than a connected narrative of the march. These letters contain many items of interest, and form the best connecting link with Springfield. Some of them are from two young officers whom I had long known in their families at New York, part addressed to me, and part to private friends, who kindly placed them at my disposal.

"JEFFERSON CITY, Oct. 4, 1862.

". . . . Night before last, Major Frank White and Jack were called from their beds to 'saddle and away' with important orders. No sooner were they gone, and I fairly settled again, sleepily glad that it wasn't I, than the alarm was beat, or rather sounded in camp. Now those persevering buglers practise the alarm all day long in the woods about camp; and I am compelled to say that its repetition at midnight startled nobody, except the Guard, who were in the saddle almost instantly. As for the Staff, they slumbered in sweet security, until the gallant Zagonyi went round to every tent, putting in his head and saying, 'Gentlemen, it is the alarm! You will please to get up in one minute!'

"At this we jumped up. What was my consternation to find that the boys had 'taken their pick' of boots and spurs when they went, leaving me with one odd boot. But there was no time to lose; so

I rushed out into the parade-ground, with a slipper on the other foot. The General stood, silent and courteous, before his tent, and received our reports. I kept my best foot foremost, and escaped notice in the dark. Some slight disturbance had occasioned the alarm; but the General wished to try the Staff and Guard. —— and —— did not get up at all. I think they had the best of it, unless the General may have noticed their absence, in which case they may be sure they are 'down a peg,' and won't recover it very soon. Well, we all went to bed, and reveille awoke us at four.

"Last night, Jack and I were called to write despatches and then carry them. The orders were no less than *march at daylight!* to many of the troops. The General has a penchant, which I regard with unaffected hostility, for writing orders at 1 A. M., and sending them as soon as the ink is dry. It is true, he is safe from rebel spies by this means; but consider the unpleasant position in which it places a merely ornamental young gentleman, who, being deceived by the Public Press, thought that Frémont's aids had nothing to do but look their prettiest and draw their pay. I am sorry to say that neither of these interesting occupations lies open to us. Instead thereof, the most abominable night-rides, over roads that yawn with chasms and are red with bottomless mud, past sentinels who invariably cock the gun, aim at your head, and put finger to the trigger when they challenge you, in vain search after mythic camps. Alas! couldn't the General have arranged the Art of War so as to omit rainy nights and keep a fellow comfortable!

"At all events, it was very comfortable to get back to bed, towards morning. Before we could fall asleep, however, the rattle of the 'long roll' on the hills around showed that the orders were beginning to work. The Staff was thoroughly aroused. Several came to our tent, to know if we could explain the rumpus. Alarm beating, men under arms, cooks lighting their fires, and all the signs of the dickens to pay. We pretended great ignorance, — said it was only a *drum*-alarm, and had nothing to do with our camp, which answers to the bugle. It was amusing to see the very ones who lay abed the night before, now so lively about nothing at all.

"This morning by seven, the white

tents which so thickly studded the hills were gone, and nothing to be seen but men marching, or sitting around their fires, drinking their morning coffee.

"The General has ordered strong coffee to the troops every morning at daylight. It not only keeps off ague, but warms them up, and puts them in good humor."

---

"Camp Asboth, near Tipton,
"Oct. 9, 3 p. m.

". . We are encamped about a mile beyond the town, the neighborhood of which shows more the gathering of an army by a great deal than you saw at Jefferson City. Where we camped last night, at California, the country round is all secession; but a few miles this side we fell into an enthusiastic loyal population, who came out along the road to express their pleasure at our coming. About this town there is more secession again, but the rebel part have mostly left. Price is still retreating. . . .

"I am endeavoring hard to get the army a little better equipped. I had hoped to get the arms, a portion of which are being altered at Cincinnati, and some more sabres. In many things Captain McKeever and Captain Callender have worked very efficiently to aid me, and we shall be much better equipped than I had hoped. The army is in the best kind of spirits, and before we get through I will show you a little California* practice, that is, if we are not interrupted. I think we can do something good.

* In allusion to the fine marching of the California Battalion in 1845–46.

". . . I want very much to see Captain Foote if he is in St. Louis. If not, I will write him by —— ——.

". . . . I send you Whittier's lines. What a fine illustration might be made of them. The rice-field with its accessories, the slaves at work, and the raised and listening heads as they first catch the sounds from far off. Be of good heart,— we are fulfilling the task allotted to us, and we will try to do it bravely. . . . .

"Our force about the State begins to work well. When the alarm came to me yesterday about Hermann, I was able to assemble men around it so quickly that there must have been three thousand three hundred there this morning, and this evening seven hundred more of cavalry in rear of rebels, and Wyman. with thirteen hundred more available. So there would have been no clamor about reënforcements. After a few weeks in the field, this will be one of the finest armies in the world.

. . . . . .

"J. C. F."

---

"Camp Asboth, 10th.

". . . I received this morning —— ——'s despatch informing me that the Secretary at War and General Thomas will be in St. Louis to-day. I am going on with formation of the plan I had indicated to you in my letter of yesterday. What the full plan is, I will let you know by sure hand, and will also inform —— ——, so that you and he may work together in aid of it. All this, provided I am not interfered with. General Price is on the Osage, pretty high up, retreating towards the south. His object is to effect junction with McCullough. That is, he says so. But in my judgment he intends retreating into Arkansas. McCullough, I am sure, is not in Missouri. We are having a severe rain-storm. . . .

" J. C. F."

---

" Camp Asboth,<br>
" 1 <i>h</i>. 40 <i>m</i>., 10th Oct.</div>

I have written you lots of scraps to-day. It is raining and storming hard, but the rain does not delay us much, for the railroad serves nearly as well as in fine weather, and I am getting a chance to get from below what little transportation means we have on hand. This makes our great difficulty. . .

I want the Secretary at War to put

an end to that kind of action which is impeding me by producing want of confidence. I think —— —— is not friendly to me, and therefore I have a right to demand that he be at once removed from my department. I think he has been purposely sent with the object, that being unfriendly he would embarrass me. I ought not to have impediments — circumstances always bring enough necessarily. . . . . .

"J. C. F."

---

"Camp Asboth, near Tipton,
"Oct. 10, 1861.

"It being a rainy day, a leisure day, and not my day to swear, I am in a fit mood to remember your kind request, and report to you concerning the various little incidents and accidents of the march and bivouac, which give on the whole a truer picture of us than documents and despatches by the score. Behold me, therefore, seated on my bed (!) lifting my heels at intervals from the wet ground, muffled in a great overcoat, and writing on my knees.

"Let me plunge at once *in medias res.* The first day's ride was delightful, even to the heavy men. They were all rejoiced, at the end of nine miles, when we stopped for the night, to find how well they bore 'the hardships of a soldier's life.' Our first camp was pitched in a swamp, for the same reason why John went to a certain place — 'because there was much water there.' Captain Haskell, who selected the ground, said water was a great thing. It is the unanimous opinion of the 'Adlati' that water is a very large thing indeed; and not a pleasant bedfellow. The fever-and-ague has made its appearance in camp already; and those preserved strawberries, put up by the 'United Society of Shakers' begin to bear an ominous significance.

"The next morning, who should appear, careering about the field, but Wamba,* mounted on a fiery horse whose paces he was exhibiting. It is my private impression that Wamba is made of wood — head and all; and having been wound up to go as an infantry corporal, his machinery cannot be altered until he is made an infantry spiritual and angelic. On the present occasion he assumed, in

* Wamba was an old regular, on duty as the General's orderly. His blue uniform, with lighter blue chevrons and stiff leather stock, suggested woad-dyeing and serf collar, and got him his sobriquet.

spite of the interpolated horse, the complete 'position of a soldier: head erect, eyes front, hand grasping the seam of the pantaloons, palm forward, heels more or less apart, feet at a strong divergent angle,' &c. The noble steed himself caught the spirit of the occasion, fancied himself in the ranks, and considered Wamba an Enfield, which it was his business alternately to 'ground' and 'shoulder' with all possible speed. To complete the picture, General Asboth and 'The General' stood in front of their tents witnessing the display. At its close, Gen. A. said benevolently, 'Ah, my dear, I see you are not Cavalerist!' and General Frémont laughed more heartily than I have ever seen him before: — at which Wamba was overcome with delight, and interjected a salute between two bounds of his horse.

Such was Camp Lovejoy. We have played upon the Colonel's generosity and innocence, until we convinced him that it was 'the correct thing' for him to send round wine in honor of the naming of our second camp after him — whence the claret already mentioned. . . .

"Alas! what am I writing! Who knows but I shall be 'jugged' for 'conduct unbecoming,' &c. &c. The colonels and majors and captains are all my superior officers; and hereafter I shall not even have the poor consolation of seeing how they ride, for last night came the terrible order that the Staff shall ride two and two, according to rank. This puts a half-dozen of captains between Jack and me, and sets me back among the unknown. Wretched me! . . . .

"The insane passion for riding six

abreast in narrow or muddy roads, which seems to seize all the junior members of the Staff, has led to this new arrangement, which Jack and I, I believe, were the first to suggest, although it results in separating us. Hereafter, each man is doomed to one neighbor, and no variety in conversation. The list is made out in the order; and after enumerating the larger animals, two and two, as Noah did, closes with 'Lt. R., &c.' Now wasn't it cruel to make me ride with, '&c.'? Who the fellow is, I don't know, but I have a horrid intuition that it is the man with a mule!* Would you believe it? Colonel Eaton brought this document of doom to our tent, last night, and I was detailed to go from tent to tent, and read

* A surgeon's assistant, who had not been able to obtain a horse, in the hurry of departure.

it to the Staff! 'O torture most refined!' . . . .

"There is a report here that the enemy is trying to get away, but cannot cross the Osage River. This is jolly, if true, and indicates a speedy chance of battle. The worst of it is, we are not in the advance, and don't seem likely to be.

"The General looks well, and I think enjoys himself much better than in Oriental St. Louis. By the way, I hear that mule is to be ordered out of the Staff, because it savors of 'Oriental Pomp.' The Queen of Sheba and the Khan of Tartary, together with Shahs, Pashas, Effendi and Howadji innumerable, rode or ride on mules. Mules being, therefore, Oriental, let their tribe be confined to the 'Eastern Department!'

"But 'Adl.' H. desires room for a line

of postscript. He has gone to town in rain and rage; for he found, on calling for his gray, that the stupid groom had fed another gray horse by mistake, and his had had nothing. Jack had finished his anathemas for the day; but I went out to help him, and we issued extra rations in honor of the occasion." . .

"R."

---

"Camp Asboth, 11th Oct. 1861.

"Captain Foote, —— and —— have arrived. —— goes down to-night and will see you in the morning. . . .

"I don't think my despatch to General Cameron, requesting McKinstry to be left with me, reached him. Whether detained by ——, or some one about him, he can find out. General Thomas, contrary to usage and regulation, ordered

McKinstry and others from my department, without doing it through me — entirely overlooking and slighting me. It is a discourtesy and military offence. General Cameron ought to come here and see the army. . . . . . Officers were also detached by the Secretary of the Navy from gun-boats, and not done through me. . . . .

"I have placed Captain Foote in charge of all the boats belonging to the flotilla. My plan is New Orleans straight; — Foote to join on the river below. I think it can be done gloriously, especially if secret can be kept. . . . It would precipitate the war forward and end it soon and victoriously.

"Talk freely with ———, Captain Foote, and ———. All are true. . . .

"J. C. F."

"Camp Asboth,
"Oct. 12, 9½ o'clock.

". . . . There is nothing to be said in addition to what I wrote yesterday, because everything in my mind is at a stand-still, until I know what result the visit of the Secretary leaves. You don't seem to feel very decided as to what course the Secretary may take, but in any event don't be in the least discouraged. If we go on from here, we shall do well. If interfered with, w shall do well in another way, but I shall act with equal decision in either case. So don't feel in the least dispirited; but bear in mind all the time that General Thomas is my enemy. He is one of those who opposed my appointment, and I am told indulged in some of the abusive and false language, which a certain class about Washington had habitually permitted to themselves in reference to me. As I told you he has conducted himself discourteously to me in his communications in reference to the army. . .

"J. C. F."

---

"Tuesday Morning, 15th Oct.
"Camp Zagonyi.

". . . . You need not be alarmed at my movements southward. They will be well considered, and you must just give me what aid you can. . . . .

"I am about nine miles out on the road to Osage River, and push right forward to-day. Our force is in splendid condition. I intend to unite together all my scattered forces, and make my army such that it can go anywhere — that is, if we are not interrupted, and of that I suppose we shall learn within a week. Consult fully and freely with Mr. ———. Keep your health good, and don't get agitated. . . . You say well that we are contending for honor and honorably; our opponents for base ends and basely. I want this little note to go to you freighted only with pleasant thoughts, a harbinger of success, and meetings soon to come. One of our little white butterflies came flying around in front of my horse as I rode along with the Secretary at War to the review at Syracuse. — This reminds me that I have not yet read the letters from the Mariposas; I will to-night. . . Thank you for the sabres and guns; send any such things forward as best you can.*

.   .   .   .   .

"J. C. F."

* Perhaps I should explain, that the frequent reference

of official work to my care came not merely from Mr. Frémont's long habit of referring all manner of work and duties to me as acting principal in his absence, but because nearly all the General's reliable officers were with him. Of those remaining, his quartermaster became ill of fever, and was in a critically dangerous state from the time of the army's leaving. The adjutant, Captain McKeever, who was very active and thorough in his attention to his duties, had his right arm disabled by a relapse of injuries received at Bull Run, causing several times so much fever and suffering as to leave actually no other head than myself; for Colonel Fiala also became ill, and even when he was well, General Curtis would not reply to any communication from him. Knowing I was always at the house, and that anything requiring attention would be sure to receive it, night or day, the General wrote to me for what was needed; and many a despatch was sent, and combination made at the bedside of invalids too worn to sit up. Of course the regular official orders came also, but in this I have only quoted from private and personal papers.

## VII.

### THE BUILDING OF THE BRIDGE.

"Warsaw, Wednesday Morning.

". . . We are all well, and the army in good spirits, notwithstanding the rain. Nothing can stand before this little army; and if not interfered with, it will do some good work. But the constant expectation of being turned off from our plans by the Department, annoys, and takes away much of the interest. I judge that the enemy is much demoralized, and much of his force will leave him, if we get nigh enough to have any effect. . . . .

"J. C. F."

"Camp on the Banks of the Osage,
"October 18, Noon.

" I crossed the river this morning, and have just returned to this side, where is my own camp. All of Sigel's that is here is already across. We have just commenced a bridge, which, by to-morrow night, will be ready for the passage of the divisions as they come up. Meantime, Sigel's and Asboth's will be over, and we shall be scouring the country in the direction of the enemy. Our difficulty consists absolutely and only in the want of transportation. On account of this the other divisions are *collées* to the line of the railroad. Ask Captain McKeever to do all that is humanly possible to get wagons, mules, harness, and drivers sent forward to Tipton. Meantime, I will seize everything of the kind there is in the country. The spirit of the men is something extraordinary; they will at once overcome anything they come in contact with. But we must get our army together. It won't do to risk too much. . .

"I understand, from other sources, that a contract made by Captain Haines, for the supply of cattle to this army, has been annulled. We are thus thrown on our own resources; but this does not at all annoy me. If it is intended to cripple me, it can't be done. When I am left to my own resources I have no fears. The transportation business troubles me the most, because it keeps back the other parts of the army, and produces delay. ——— can tell you if this is done purposely. . .

"J. C. FREMONT."

"Banks of the Osage,
"October 19, 8 a. m.

"Held back by want of transportation, I have not been able to get the army nigh enough to the enemy to strike a blow, and so I lose a victory. I crossed the river yesterday afternoon, with part of the Guard, and sent them forward with some of Waring's cavalry. They may do a little something to put a white mark on the day. Hunter's, Pope's, and McKinstry's divisions are still alongside the railroad, transportation bound. But we are not losing time. Bridge-building, and scouring the country, gathering in teams and provisions, &c., all advance the work; and the moment I can move I will do it with effect.

"Can you tell me anything about Warren's cavalry? I do not send many orders to St. Louis, because I do not feel that they have force. The course of the administration encouraged all manner of disobedience and neglect on the part of the officers there; and paymasters, quartermasters, and all, feel that my orders may be disregarded with impunity. . . ."

---

"Camp near Warsaw,
"October 17, 1861.

"As you will have seen, we have made quite a respectable distance in the pursuit, and have been rewarded here by rumors that Price is only thirty to fifty miles ahead, and waiting to give us battle;— but rumor is so unreliable.

"Three days have brought us from Tipton, about forty miles, which may be considered a pretty good start for a green army. We arrived last night, though not quite in the town, encamping about a mile north of it. While awaiting the baggage-trains, the General, calling for some 'young officers to go with him,' and a company of the Guard, galloped like fun through mud and water, and abysmal roads, to the high bluffs of the Osage River, passing through the town on the way. Before getting to the village, we met General Sigel, with his adjutant. He had been here all day, slowly putting his brigade across on one small ferry-boat. He rode with us through Warsaw, and we, 'from her heights, surveyed' the river which Price had to run around to avoid thrashing, and which we are about to cross in order to thrash him after all.

"Having seen the possibilities of crossing, we rode back to camp,—the soldiers of Sigel's command filling the air with cheers and welcoming shouts for our chief. We had a pleasant enough night, and this morning the tents were struck, and we all moved over to the heights above the river.

"While camp was being pitched, we rode with the General to the ferry, where he remained some time consulting Captain Pike, the engineer who is to put the bridge through. 'Now, Captain,' asked the General, 'how many hours do you propose to use in bridging this river?' 'It depends upon how many men I may have, sir. If I have enough, you shall cross by two o'clock to-morrow.' I am afraid the entire lack of tools and lumber will put the Captain out in his calculations, but we shall see. Pike will do his best. The General certainly puts men to their trumps. . . .

"H."

"CAMP NEAR WARSAW,
"October 19, 1861.

". . . . . We have now got well to work upon the bridge. R. has been doing good service in the lumber department; the north side material being improvised from the *débris* of log-houses and barns, sacrificed for the occasion, the south side cut and hauled from the virgin forest. I had been variously employed all the morning, writing and riding for the General; in the afternoon, he took part of the Body-Guard and went out on a little reconnoissance across the river. As he rode off he sent me down to help Captain Pike. 'See that he has all he wants; let there be no hitch;—see that everything *moves*.'

"So down I went, and having a roving commission, became a sort of 'Jack-at-all-trades,' putting in wherever it seemed necessary, impressing teams and drivers, getting tools, ropes, and necessary articles, directing the pioneers in the woods where and what to cut, hauling the timber from the woods, &c., &c. Pike with his efficient assistants, Shepley and Kern, were down on the bank, directing the busy workmen, and shaping the rough hewn trestles, measuring and cutting stringer and brace, fixing rope and chain and bolt, and putting through the more important preparatory work. Lieutenant Waring was in the woods, which rang with the axes of his pioneers, and the shouts of his teamsters, detachments from the 'fancy Body-Guard,' serving extempore in both capacities. And Colonel Shanks, M. C. and A. D. C.,—the indomitable, indefatigable, and tremendous,—was everywhere, driving, cutting, working in a manner wonderful to behold. Now in the forest, showing the workmen how to put the ox-chain on a log and 'snake' it through the brush; now knee-deep in the river, swearing at reluctant 'Dutchmen'; now driving an ox-team along the dusty road;—always efficiently at work, helping all, interfering with none. This, on the southern bank. The other side saw Raymond inexorably pulling down houses, barns, sheds, stables, — anything that could furnish the proper length and size of timber for this all-devouring bridge; impressed teams hauling the materials to the bank; refractory mules kicking and plunging in the water while taking the various necessaries to the central island; quiet groups of steady-handed Germans getting the logs and planks ready to be put together in shape;

in short it was as thorough a specimen of hearty, earnest, well-put work as one could wish to see.

"Meantime, I was wandering about, a kind of odd wheel, but managing to 'turn up' in the right place with such frequency as to keep me from being too lazy. Among other things, tools and spikes were needed. What easier than to gallop over to the town, get them and send them back in some unlucky wagon which should chance to be near? Well, I have seen easier things. Armed with the Provost Marshal's pass, I had to go into every store, question and cross-examine the secesh owner who 'didn't care to sell,' and 'didn't know what he'd got;' root and ransack in every corner, trip and stumble through every cellar, over barrels and kegs innumerable; and finally, for my pains, had scraped together a few augers, one or two sledges, half a dozen chisels, and — no more! Then spikes were needed. Surely spikes are common enough in a frontier town. Vain hope! They must be created. Clothed with plenary powers by the General, I was to take any forge and set to work any smith, — for The Bridge was all-important.

"I went to one large forge with four fires, where about fifty horses were waiting and being shod, and to the infinite disgust of the various regiments whose horses were there, to the surprise of all the smiths, and with some explanation to their independent Western minds, that the General's order must pass over all others, I 'seized' the fires, and set the men all at hammering out my spikes. The iron I had to find like the tools, in warehouse, cellar, barn, or store, or wherever it was to be found.

"Thus, between forest, river, and town, I had to be lively. After supper I went down again, and saw them working by moonlight and firelight. That was a picture! A gleaming fire at the foot of the dark, high, wooded bluff! The low, sandy island, far off and indistinct in the moonlight; the rushing river between, and this wild, solitary scene, made more weird and even more solitary by the busy groups of excited, earnest men. The shouting of voices, the clangor of blows, the creaking of ropes, and rattling of chains, mingled with the noise of the river, and occasionally when the grotesque, wide-spreading form of one of the huge trestles had been successfully lowered into the swift blackness of the water, the long, loud shout of triumph drowned all else. But you will weary of all this detail, and I must get sleep for to-morrow's work. . . .

"H."

---

"BANKS OF THE OSAGE,<br>
"Oct. 19, 1861, late in the afternoon.

"Thank you for your pleasant letters of encouragement, especially for that one which points to the future crowning result, if God wills it so. And as events seem to have pointed out the way, I will keep my eyes steadily fixed in that direction until the flag which floats above our army glows in the "insufferable light."

"I put this letter of yours with Mr. ———'s, which reflects the color of my mind. They will keep my mind alive and vigilant and true to the great end which I shall now always see before me.

"I was made happy by finding Mr. —— and Mr. —— as I rode into camp to-day. They were like home faces and trusty friends, full of pleasure to see, after the close contest with enemies which I have been waging. I have arranged with them to hurry up my supplies and transportation the best they can, and I am sure they will do all that under the circumstances is humanly possible, and with their aid I shall be able to do what I wish. I have from Captain Foote himself, and from them, better hopes for his coöperation than you were able to give in your letter of Tuesday evening. Don't fear; if this thing is destined to be done, all will go right with us here. I shall keep my communications open, and will be able to give you intelligence of my movements, and at the same time, to hear from you, and keep informed of the enemy's movements on the Mississippi. I wrote to-day to General Smith. The guns destined for Price will never reach him, if I get my transportation in time. General Prentiss I shall be glad to see. I will send him directions when I get a little farther along. Day by day I will send you some little slip of what I want done. I begin to feel stronger. It pleases me to see how kindly disposed the people are to me, and how much trust they place in me. I did not know, until I received your letters to-day, what was the cause of the reinforcements being sent to Ironton. Tell Captain McKeever that his promptitude gives me pleasure. His dispositions were excellent, and the effect may reach farther than shows at first; still, as soon as the regiments can be spared and equipped with transportation,

I want them hurried up in this direction, for the reason that, in certain contingencies, we should be beyond reach of reinforcements, and obliged to rely on ourselves alone.

"Zagonyi got no action, but brought back some useful spoils,— horses, wagons, cattle, provisions, &c. . . . .

"J. C. F."

(ZAGONYI SPEAKING.)

"On the 18th of October about fifty men, personally with the General, crossed the Osage to have a little observation of the enemy on the other side. The General found out, through talking with citizens, that a body of men were starting to the rebel army, about twenty-two miles from Warsaw, on the Osceola road, south. He at once ordered me to proceed in the night to find out if they are there. We arrived at eleven o'clock in the night, but was too late; they left three days before, but found horses, mules, cattle, and about one hundred and twenty bushels of wheat, which we captured and handed over for General Sigel's brigade use. We left camp about four or five in the evening, arrived back next day about eleven — forty-five miles — without a bite of bread or meat, but a little mush made by ourselves at one in the night out of the captured corn flour; we found some salt and a little molasses, — not I, but the others, did like and eat it. The horses had everything. But we did not have a blanket with us. It was so that we went out only to see the country, but finding on our way about these rebels so near, we went after them without turning back to make any preparation. The General sent for a company of Frémont Hussars to accompany us; he did not leave us until they came up."

---

"Banks of Osage,
"Oct. 20, 1861 — 8 a. m.

"Mr. —— and Mr. —— are harnessing up for their return. I have had much pleasure in their visits and the favorable impressions they have in regard to our present struggle. But the aspect I suppose will change from day to day, dependent upon what we may do in the field, and this depends upon our supplies. The army in Kentucky, and this one in the field should, *without loss of an hour*, be strongly and efficiently reinforced. In this way the war can be terminated this winter; and it is treason to the country to put in peril the great stake at issue for the purpose of gratifying private vengeance against an individual. Forward movements now, and no more trifling with the war and with the blood and treasure of the country. The mercantile interest of the nation demands peace, and it may be had by spring.

" Say to Colonel Koerner that I have not a moment to write this morning. I will write to him. Meantime, thank him very warmly for his exertions in Illinois, and for their prompt result;—two regiments make a great acquisition just now. Ask him to continue for the present to work upon this project, and I will give him my ideas later. Thank him, too, for his despatch to the President respecting the pay of the officers. What reason can there be for not paying them except to discredit me? The President said he would confirm my appointments, and they were made accordingly;

what then is the meaning of the order not to pay them? —— is here. I will write you his intelligence if I have time. . .

"What I have just learned from —— satisfies me that we can easily carry out what I have told you above, and depend on it if I am not interrupted, the victory is ours, thoroughly and entirely. Send me transportation, and I will go ahead " like a house on fire." . . . .

"Send me forward all the regiments possible. Arm them with the Austrian musket as altered by Greenwood. We are receiving them at the arsenal at the rate of five hundred a day. In my judgment the enemy is greatly disconcerted by the taking of Paducah, and our movements here and the lower country. New Madrid and Memphis are open to us. Send the transportation, and send the regiments. . . .

"J. C. F."

"WARSAW,
"Oct. 22, 1861.

".. Our army is sadly in want of transportation. The Department has been so crippled that the necessary wagons and teams could not be furnished; and now we are on the verge of starvation — *i. e.*, living on beef and salt — while plenty of commissary stores are at Tipton, fifty-five miles from here. In order to get more wagons, the baggage of the army is to be reduced to the ultimate minimum. The General sets the example, sending back his mess-chest and trunk. We shall follow his example, and leave behind our camp beds, and all superfluous baggage. It's precious little I have to spare; but I think I can bid a short farewell to clean linen, and reduce my table-equipage to the beef-pan and the salt-box. My dress-uniform must go, if I have to carry it under my arm; for we are bound to have a triumphal entry and a Thanksgiving-Dinner at Memphis, to be followed up by a Christmas at New Orleans. Government must also furnish transportation for my meerschaum. It is coloring successfully. I shall make my first charge with it between my teeth — breathing fire and smoke. The whole army has been rejoiced by the discovery at this place of a large quantity of salt and tobacco — especially the latter. One plug has been issued to each man, to supply the lack of things to eat; and the gallant host sends up but one voice: "Give us the luxuries of life, and we'll do without its necessaries." And the luxury we most desire can be had without money, but not without Price.

"R."

"WARSAW, Mo.,
"Oct. 22, 1861.

". . . . . Ros and I have been for the last three days very busy helping Captain Pike with his bridge. Ros being detailed to the duty one day ahead of me, had charge of the department of supplying lumber for the north side of the bridge, and he put it through well. The General sent me to keep a general look-out, and see that there was no hitch, that everything went smoothly.

"Major Frank White is just in, having made a *détour* from Georgetown, and with his one hundred and eighty men surprised and driven out the five hundred troops who were holding Lexington for the rebels, released the prisoners, sent them down the river, remained in possession twenty-four hours and more, and escaping by night through the cordon which had surrounded him, marched down to us in a little over three days. He made a forced march of sixty miles from Georgetown to Lexington between sunset and sunrise, and thus surprised the rebels. We are proud of our messmate and with good reason, *n'est ce pas?* He captured Jackson's Secession State flag, which he has given to me. To-morrow he is off and away to the van.

"H."

## VIII.

### OVER THE HILLS AND FAR AWAY.

"Headquarters Western Department,
"October 23.
"Camp on road three miles beyond Osage River.

"I MADE but a short camp yesterday evening, having been delayed by the numberless detentions which necessarily surround myself. So many inexperienced officers, coming to me for the merest trifles, fritters away much of my time. Our bridge will not be finished until noon to-day, and Asboth's division will consequently be delayed in its advance; but it will probably get across to-day, and meanwhile Sigel is going ahead. Tell Captain Foote to push on his preparations; it will not be long before I send his orders to him. . . . .

"To-day is bright and pleasant. When

the army leaves this it will march vigorously. We have already forced the enemy clear of nearly all the State, and our movement will effectually free the State of him for the winter. It had been his intention to overrun all North Missouri to the Mississippi and go into Iowa. When I left St. Louis a large detachment of his force had already crossed the Missouri (*vide* Sturgis's and Prentiss's despatches.) My movement towards Georgetown drew him immediately back to the south side of the river, and the forward movement of my forces put him into a retreat which he is still prosecuting. War consists not only in battles, but in well-considered movements which bring the same results. We have made many movements of this kind for which no credit has ever been given.

. . . . . .

"J. C. F."

"Camp White, near Lindley's Creek,
"October 24.

"I have just had the triumphant satisfaction to read your note, enclosing the despatch from Col. Carlin. God and events are favoring us in the great work. All along our line the "insufferable light" begins to shine. I am so sorry for him; *

---

* Col. Baker, on his way from Oregon to the Senate, made in San Francisco a farewell address. It was in October, and he was urging the people to united action in the coming Presidential election. Suddenly stopping himself, he asked why he wasted time in urging to efforts for a victory already won; — that the true subject to consider was the use to make of that victory; — he gave them a rapid *resumé* of the results of the Southern policy — its remorseless, unscrupulous manner of persecuting, even to death, men who were its powerful and successful opposers. Latest was his "murdered friend Broderick" (as Mr. Broderick himself said, "Killed because I opposed the extension of slavery and a corrupt administration"). And then came one of those perfectly beautiful and artistic passages which gave Colonel Baker his

— the way, after long waiting, was just opening. Make my warmest acknowledgments to Captain McKeever, and tell him to send them to Colonel Carlin and his command. I will write from next camp. Washington now ought to be silent. We were just starting. I sent the despatch to the sharpshooters (Major Holman), and their answering shout just now comes to me. I send it also to Zagonyi (getting ready to start on the road below me). Major White made a bold and handsome dash into Lexington. I will send his report from next camp. We are six miles north of Quincy; Sigel ahead, Asboth

deserved fame as an orator — closing with a picture of Liberty hunted, imprisoned, bound to the stake, her very ashes scattered to the winds. "I looked again, and I beheld her, throned on high, her garments white and shining, and in her strong right hand the sword of Freedom, red with '*insufferable light.*'"

next behind. I have a good letter from General McKinstry. He is pressing forward; his advance will be in Warsaw to-day. Every way we are doing well. . .

"J. C. F."

---

"In the Field, near Humansville,
"October 25, 1861.

". . . I came on this morning with a few of the Guard, Holman's sharp-shooters, and the Benton Cadets; and, for the time, my headquarters constitute the extreme advance of the army. Gen. Sigel's cavalry advance has just passed, and his division will be encamped to-night four miles ahead of me. Gen. Asboth's division is on the march, and will encamp to-night seven miles in my rear, on an open prairie country, around which a wooded creek sweeps. This would afford room for an army of forty thousand to encamp, and here perhaps the divisions which are behind, — Hunter's, Pope's, and McKinstry's, — will concentrate. General McKinstry is doing his best to get forward, and so, I suppose, are all now.

"I was encamped on a farm-ground, only seven miles in the rear, last night, at a very pretty place. From there I sent forward Zagonyi with nearly all the Guards, together with Major White's command, all under the command of Zagonyi. They left at night on an expedition, of which I will send you results when I hear.

"Generally, I think we are doing well. Our forward march here has been conducted with all the rapidity possible, and we have scoured the country broadly as we advanced; and, in my judgment, our whole movement can be characterized as very successful. Joined to the success at Ironton,—Missouri, it seems to me, stands out in vigorous relief.

"We are anxious to know how affairs progress around the Potomac. The slip you sent me announcing the death of Colonel Baker, had not the result of the engagement at Poolesville. . . . .

"To-morrow we expect a mail through from St. Louis. . . . . . . . .

"In reply to Kœrner's telegram to the President, about the pay of officers appointed by me, I notice that the Assistant Secretary of War calls these appointments '*these irregularities,*' and says they will be corrected at the earliest moment. They were not irregularities, as we know. They were authorized by the President, and, therefore, strictly regular. But he may rest assured that the time for correction will certainly come. But I don't think much of them now, and they have lost the power to sting. . . . . .

"Charley is well; he is all right now.* He messes with me, and sleeps in my ambulance (the chariot and four), and, with a buffalo robe and two blankets, has the most comfortable kind of quarters.

. . . . . . .

"J. C. F."

---

* He had been kicked by a horse. Charley was my oldest boy, — only ten years old; but he quoted "Casabianca" as a precedent, and carried his point of going with his father. Major Zagonyi had been good enough to let him drill with the Guard, and although, of course, only an "honorary member," he wore the uniform and did some of the duties of a sergeant. When the Secretary of War reviewed the troops at Syracuse, Charley went through the review with great credit to his training. It was no small test to go successfully through a real review as part of several thousand cavalry.

"In the Field near Humansville,
"October 25, — 7½ p. m.

"I shall have news of a little action to give you by next express. I sent forward Zagonyi to strike a blow yesterday evening. I just received a despatch from him, informing me that the enemy has been reënforced at the particular point very considerably; still, he goes on, and asks for reënforcements to be sent. He was but eight miles from the enemy when he wrote to me, at half-past eleven this morning; it is now eight (evening). He went right on, and, I am afraid, will be rash. I sent immediately forward eight hundred cavalry and a section of artillery. By next express I will inform you. . .

"J. C. F."

(ZAGONYI SPEAKING.)

"Just as we arrived in the camp, Yost's Station, October 24, I heard from some scouts that there were three or four hundred rebels in Springfield. I at once reported myself at the General's tent, and asked for permission to go forward. The General did not want to grant it directly; he promised me that after another day's march will let me. He considered it too far to go from that place. I retired, but in half an hour reported myself again, begging for permission, trying to make the General believe that if he don't let me go they will run away from our approach; remarking, with respect, that if he don't let me go, next morning he won't find me in the camp — that I will run away in the night. At last he gave his permission, if I take some additional help. I told that plenty, enough, my own command; but obeyed the orders, that it shall not be countermanded. We started at about nine o'clock in the evening. Before starting, I intended to leave one officer in command with the remaining of my command. It was a difficult work to select one. Trusting in one's quiet nature, Lieut. Kennedy, I gave him the orders to remain behind in command. With tears in his eyes begged me not to leave him behind; he would consider that I did not put trust in him to go into the battle if I did not let him go along. But in the same time obeyed the orders. Half an hour later reported myself to the General before starting, and asked his permission not to leave my officer behind — none of them is willing to remain. The General gave his hearty consent, and congratulated my officers and men that they are so willing to see the enemy.

"It was done quietly, so that the enemy should not hear of it; but the men were very much rejoiced that the long promised time came.

"It was a cold night; they shivered, poor fellows, and it was a little bit of rain on us during the night — there was not an overcoat in the Guard; but we made twenty-five miles from nine till five, A. M. From five till half-past six we took a little rest, having a little cold meat in our haversack. For seven days we had had nothing but meat, without salt; but still knowing we could do no better, there was no complaint. My scout found me a secession house, where we had plenty of sheaf-oats and hay." (I suggested they also could have had something to eat — " Was no time in a small family to bake bread " — what there was they did get, but it was of no value.)

"Started from there, and arrived at half-past eleven — eight miles from Springfield — seventeen miles. Here we found out that the enemy is eighteen or nineteen hundred strong. From this place I wrote despatch to General Frémont and General Sigel."

(Among other "asides," I preserved the following, as exemplifying his inability to see what constituted "rashness.")

"They call it a 'rash act.' How is it possible to say it so? From half-past eleven till half-past four we knew we were to meet nineteen hundred men (but in reality twenty-two hundred), was time enough to reconsider and cool down every rashness. Blood cools in five hours. It is so. Very naturally it could not be '*rashness.*'"

(COPY FROM ORIGINAL IN PENCIL.)

"12 o'clock, A. M., 8 miles from Springfield, October 25, 1861.

"General: —

"The information on which I can rely is, that Wednesday evening fifteen hundred men came in Springfield, — and that at present there is not less than eighteen or nineteen hundred men. — I march forward and will try what I can do — in the same time I would be thankful if some reinforcement could come after me. Should I be successful I need them to hold the place, should I be defeated to have some troops to fall back with my worn-out command.

"I will report shortly again.

"With high respect,
"Chs. Zagonyi,
"*Major Comm. Body Guard.*
"To Maj.-Gen. J. C. Frémont,
"*Comm. West. Dept.*"

(COPY.)

"HEADQUARTERS WESTERN DEPARTMENT,
"October 25, — 7½ P. M.

"Your despatch is received. I send to you Colonel Carr with strong force of cavalry and some artillery. I will send more if you need it. Let me know immediately.

(Signed) "J. C. FRÉMONT,
"*Maj.-Gen. Com.*

"To Maj. ZAGONYI,
"*Commanding Expedition to Springfield.*"

---

(COPY.)

"HEADQUARTERS OF THE 3D DIV. D. OF THE W.
"CAMP 10 MILES FROM BOLIVAR, Oct. 25, 1861.

"To Major ZAGONYI, near Springfield: —

"If there are eighteen hundred or nineteen hundred men at Springfield with the intention to resist you, I advise you *not* to make an attack against the town, but to watch the enemy and attack him when he *leaves* the town, which he will do, as soon as we *approach* Springfield.

"I do not believe that the company or two of cavalry now under my command will be of great use to you, as they are not well prepared and have no sabres, but I will advance them nevertheless as soon as possible, to join you and to give you assistance in case you should be repulsed.

"The most necessary thing and your object should be, to send good and reliable information to us and to attack the enemy only in case you find him in a condition or in a position where you can with great probability defeat him instead of being defeated.

"Two hundred men like yours can do wonders; but to attack a town with cavalry only, when the enemy is prepared to receive them, is always a very critical thing.

"I send to General Frémont and will wait for his orders.

"Yours Respectfully,

(Signed) "F. SIGEL,

"Act. Major-Gen'l com'd'g 3d Div.

"N B.—The troops under my command cannot be in the neighborhood of Springfield before two days, except the cavalry, which can move quicker. Send me news as quickly as possible."

---

(COPY.)

"BY TELEGRAPH FROM ROLLA,
"29th, 1861.

"To Captain McKEEVER:—

"Ambulances just arrived from Springfield. Left Thursday night. Colonel Taylor with all his force left Springfield Friday, 18th inst. Colonel Frazier with one thousand men came into Springfield Friday the 25th. He is after three hundred sacks of salt taken from McClurg. Is pushing everything and ready to leave any moment. Reports Price at —— (telegraph blunder over name) Newton County; reports all rebels leaving for Arkansas; also reports Generals Frémont and Sigel at Bolivar.

"This despatch gives the rebel force under Colonel Taylor and Colonel Frazier.

"G. W. DODGE,
" Col. Comm'd'g Post at Rolla."

## IX.

### SPRINGFIELD.

(Zagonyi.)

"After a brief stay we marched very slowly to give time to my scout to bring me the best information from Springfield, which he did about one o'clock that the rebels hardly will face me, but will run. To meet them sure I left the Bolivar road, crossed over to the Osceola road, and from there to the Mount Vernon. In case they should retreat, to be before them. (Major White's command with me all this time. I left the big road at two and one-half hours. He should have been at most at twelve hours with me.*)

---

\* Some misunderstanding of orders separated the

"About four o'clock I arrived on the highest point on the Ozark mountains. Not seeing any sign of the enemy, I halted my command, made them known that the enemy instead of four hundred is nineteen hundred. But I promised them victory if they will be what I thought and expected them to be. If any of them too much fatigued from the fifty-six miles, or sick, or unwell, to step forward; but nobody was worn out. (Instead of worn out, it is true that every eye was a fist big.) I made them known that this day I want to fight the first and the last hard battle, so that if they meet us again they shall know with who they have to do and remember the Body-Guard. And ordered quick march.

commands before the Charge,— although, unknown to the Guard, the Prairie Scouts did brave and efficient fighting on a distant part of the field.

"Besides, I tell them whatever we meet, to keep together and look after me; would I fall, not to give up, but to avenge mine death. To leave every ceremonious cuts away in the battle-field and use only right cut and thrust. Being young, I thought they might be confused in the different cuts, and the Hungarian hussars say, " Never defend yourselves, — better make your enemy defend himself and you go in." I just mention them that you know very well that I promised you that I will lead you shortly to show that we are not a fancy and only guard-doing-duty soldiers, but fighting men."

---

"My despatch meant what I will do. In the hour I get the news my mind was settled. I say, Thank God, if I am to fight, it is not four hundred! but nineteen hundred!

"I halt my men again and say, Soldiers! When I was to recruit you, I told you you was not parade soldiers, but for war. The enemy is more than we. The enemy is two thousand and we are but one hundred and fifty. It is possible no man will come back. No man will go that thinks the enemy too many. He can ride back. (I see by the glimpsing of their eye they was mad to be chanced a coward.)

"The Guard that follow me will take for battle-cry, 'Frémont and the Union and — CHARGE ——!'

'O the wild charge they made!'

"Running down the lane between the cross-fire, the first company followed close (Newhall's), but the rest stopped for a couple seconds. I had not wondered if none had come, — young soldiers and such a tremendous fire, bullets coming like a rain.

"As I arrived down on the creek I said aloud, 'If I could send somebody back I would give my life for it. We are lost here if they don't follow.' My Adjutant, Majthenyi, hearing, feared that he will be sent back, jumped down from his horse and busy himself opening the fence."

---

"I expected to find the enemy on the other end of Springfield, but, unexpectedly coming out of the woods to an open place, I was fired on in front of mine command. Halted for a minute, seeing that, or a bold forward march under a cross-fire, or a doubtful retreat with losing most of my men, I took the first, and commanded 'March!'

Under a heavy cross-fire, (in trot) down the little hill in the lane, — two hundred yards, — to a creek, where I ordered the fence to be opened — marched in my command, — ordered them to form, and with the war-cry of 'Frémont and the Union,' we made the attack. The First Company (Newhall's), forty-seven strong, against five or six hundred infantry, and the rest against the cavalry, was made so successfully, that, in three minutes, the cavalry run in every direction, and the infantry retreated in the thick wood, and their cavalry in every direction. The infantry we were not able to follow in the woods, so that we turned against the running cavalry. With those we had in different places, and in differing numbers, attacked and dispersed, — not only in one place, but our men was so much emboldened, that twenty or thirty attacked twenty, thirty times their numbers, and these single-handed attacks, fighting here and there on their own hook, did us more harm than their grand first attack. By them we lost our prisoners. Single-handed they fought bravely, specially one, — a lieutenant, — who, in a narrow lane, wanted to cut himself through about sixty of us, running in that direction. But he was not able to go very far. Firing two or three times, he ran against me, and put his revolver on my side, but, through the movement of the horse, the shot passed behind me. He was a perfect target — first cut down, and after shot. He was a brave man; for that reason I felt some pity to kill him.

"Young men was the guard — but remarkable and extraordinary it was they gone so nice through.

"In this way the town was cleared. We went to their encampment, but the ground was deserted, and we returned to the Court-house, raised the company-flag on the Court-house, liberated prisoners, and collected my forces together, — which numbered not more, including myself, than seventy men on horseback. The rest, — without horses, or wounded, and about thirty who had dispersed in pursuit of the enemy, — I could not gather up; and it was midnight before they reached me, — and some of them next day.

"I. never was sick in my life, Madame, till what time I find myself leaving Springfield, in the dark, with only sixty-nine men and officers, — I was the seventy. I was perfectly sick and disheartened, so I could hardly sit in the saddle, to think of so dear a victory.

"But it ended so that fifteen is dead, — two died after — ten prisoners, who was released, and of the wounded, not one will lose a finger. In all seventeen lost."

---

"One hundred and fifty started on the lane down. Thirty-nine or forty was disabled and thrown down — mostly horses hurt — and in the real attack was not more than one hundred and ten, — the highest number."

---

"Half the battle is won, if you go into the fight with spirit and noise, and, mostly, the enemy is disheartened by it. Very natural, going against them in fast trot, and with loud noise, they was not able to keep in order. They was not perfect soldiers, and their horses took fright, (I knew they would). Our horses was worn out, and, as general thing, our making noise did not frighten them, and our horses was more trained than theirs.

"After this we had to retire, — leave the town in the hands of those who was without any horses. I was perfectly sure that the enemy never will return, but, as a soldier, I could not risk any possibility of their return.

"My men and horses was so much worn out, they had not been able to take care of themselves, and less of a town. They were worn out, — hardly could speak, — hardly could sit in the saddle, from tiredness; arms worn from keeping the horses from excitement back, and the other hand from the use of the sword was worn out that hardly could hold up. Faces blackened from powder and dust; hungered out from five o'clock in the morning till this time, — six in the evening, — not knowing when we will have any more of anything, made them perfectly useless."

———

"As we dashed through the streets, the women came out from their houses to the gates of their gardens; waved their handkerchiefs, and brought out flags, and did not frighten them at all, — the shooting and fighting. Captain Foley exchanged words with them, — inquired if there were any rebels? Answered and told where, perfectly coolly, — was not afraid at all. Next day they took the greatest pains to attend the sick and the wounded, — bringing them every delicacy, and attending to their comfort. As we left Springfield, was already dark, that we could not see ten steps ahead.

"The bugler (Frenchman) I ordered him two three time to put his sword away and take the bugle in his hand, that I shall be able to use him. Hardly I took my eyes down, next minute I seen him, sword in the hand, all bloody; and this he done two or three times. Finally, the mouth of the bugle being shot away, the bugler had excuse for gratifying himself in use of the sword.

"One had a beautiful wound through the nose. My boy, I told him, I would give anything for that wound. After twenty-four hours it was beautiful — just the mark enough to show a bullet has passed through; but, poor fellow, he cannot even show it. It healed up so as to leave no mark at all. He had also five on his leg and shoulder, and the fifth wound he only found, after six days; he could not move easy, for that reason, he was late to find there was two wounds in the legs. In the attack, every one is worth to be mentioned. I make up my mind to name no names, when all was deserving mention.

"Lieut. Kennedy [the "quiet-natured" officer] was wounded twice, — in the arm and in the side. The surgeons said he would lose it; but he has not.

"More than sixty horses were 'bulletted;' seventeen carrying bullets were brought back to St. Louis."

Every one who followed the infantry into the wood was killed; but from another wooded place, several of the wounded were recovered. Corporal Dean, who was wounded severely in going down the lane, was thrown where he could see his riderless horse charge with the Guard. Presently the horse returned, snuffing the air, and neighing. He called it by name, when it came running to him; but, coming on the other side of the fence, after many ineffectual attempts to get to its master, it again made off to the rest.

I think Wisa was the one whose life may be said to have been saved by the little terrier. This dog had joined the Guard on one of their excursions in the outskirts of St. Louis, coming back to camp with them, and keeping with them, not only there and all the time on the march, but charging with the Guard, and keeping up in the heat of the fray. As the day closed, he found himself by this wounded man, and, nestling to him, remained by him all night — sallying out of the wood at dawn, and, by his barking and actions, inducing a man whom he met to follow him to where Wisa lay, stiff and exhausted, with pain, and cold, and hunger. "Corporal" was the name of this little fellow, and, as the Knight's dog lies at his feet on the old tombs, a terrier *couchant* should bring up this story and be its "Finis."

---

"Headquarters in the Field,
"Western Department,
"Oct. 26, 1861.

"I am really delighted this morning with Zagonyi's brilliant action, and half at least of my delight is in the pleasure it will give to you. I send Captain Howard with the despatches to Captain McKeever, that he may forward them officially to Washington.

"As I have already informed you, having learned on the 24th that three or four hundred of the enemy, with a large train, from Lebanon, were in Springfield, from which we were then forty-eight miles distant, I sent forward Major Zagonyi with one hundred and fifty of my Guards, and Major White with one hundred and eighty of his cavalry, the whole under Major Zagonyi, and with directions to disperse the enemy, take or destroy the train, and fall back upon our main body. I also ordered forward, in support, the cavalry from Wyman's command, then advancing by way of Cross Plains to Bolivar. Yesterday evening at half-past six I received the first despatch from Zagonyi informing me that the enemy had been reënforced by fifteen hundred men, but that he should go forward and attack, and asking that reënforcements should be sent to him. In half an hour it was on its way to him, and at nine o'clock left Sigel's camp, which is six miles in advance of us. The reënforcement was eight hundred cavalry and one section of artillery. This morning, before day, Mr. —— was in my tent with your letters, and while he was giving me his news, one of Zagonyi's men arrived with his despatch, giving the account of his brilliant victory. I had all along promised this fine body of young men that I would give them an early opportunity for distinction. They have profited by it well. Zagonyi, on starting from camp, had left one of his officers in charge of the few of the guards necessarily left at camp. He came to me and told me that this officer was literally crying at being left, and requested permission for him to go. Of course he went. Zagonyi gives no details, but I am afraid, from what I can learn, that I have lost fifteen of them. I will send you details. His messenger met the reënforcement about three miles beyond Bolivar. Zagonyi was falling back upon it. I am moving forward, and to-night the advance of the army will be in Springfield.

"Just at this moment I hear the shouting of the men who were drawn up to hear Zagonyi's despatch read.

"I enclose a little note to the President. Send it or not as you think fit. If you send it, mark it 'Private' on the outside.

"This was really a Balaklava charge. The Guards numbered only one hundred and fifty. You notice that Zagonyi says he has seen charges, but never such a one. Their war-cry, he says, sounded like thunder. This action is a noble example to the army.

"If you send it, take especial care that the letter to the President *certainly* reaches him.

"I will now read my letters, of which I have a large package. I just glanced over your note to get its good, bright color, and answer by next mail, knowing that this is going to give you great pleasure and confidence. . . . .

"J. C. F."

It will be remembered that the President took no active part in military matters at that time, and the allied forces who dictated on Western affairs took care that no star for merit should find its way westward.

They manage these things better in France. No French soldier felt his knapsack too empty when it carried the possible baton of a marshal. It had happened — why not to him too? — that the Emperor, passing as some heroic act was performed, detached his own cross of the Legion of Honor, and himself fastened it on the soldier's breast — or he had said *Mon brave, je te nomme Serjeant ou Capitaine*, or whatever their mind suggested as nearly fabulous. But all were sure that their names never died out; — at roll-call the living answered, for those who could speak no more, "Died on the field of honor." Courage and devotion could not go unrewarded among them. Nor does Napier, in his elaborate History of the Peninsular War, disdain to pause and record the example of the nameless private, who at the siege of Badajoz, actually ran head-foremost upon and into the palisade of sabres erected by the French.

Suppose General Jackson had been the General to whom this request for Zagonyi's promotion was referred. Our frontier Indians (who see a good deal of garrisons, and have a certain grim humor) have their own name for such officers as have not seen service. " Peace Captains" they call them. Being a frontiersman, " a civilian you know — no military education whatever, nor any of that sort of thing." General Jackson might have made an Indian's distinction in the case, and given rewards to the young heroes " red with the soldiers' true baptism of the battle-field," rather than to the correctly prepared Peace Captains.

---

"In the Field, Bolivar,
"Oct. 27, 1861.

"As I told you I intended, our advance was in Springfield last night and our flag flying there. Our troops were moving all night long on the road between this and Springfield, where I shall stop to-night.

"By Mr. ——, who goes back to-day, I send you the secession flag captured by the Guards in the action at Springfield. I rode ahead last night to a house where was Zagonyi with some of our wounded, two of whom were officers. So far as I know at this moment, our loss in killed was fifteen, but I shall know better at the close of the day. The secession loss was severe. I will give you details to-morrow. The action lasted an hour and three quarters after the first charge. The secessionists formed in line in their camp, and the Guards took down a fence under their fire before they could charge,— this, after the beginning in which the Guards received their fire, from which forty of our horses fell. One of our non-commissioned officers had three horses shot under him, others several. We are obliged to leave sixty of their horses, more or less wounded. The action was continued through the town, which was cleared street by street, the Secessionists firing also from houses, fences, and other protection. Many of the men have lost their caps, and had their clothes torn to pieces,— as Zagonyi says, 'not any more fit to appear as Body-Guard.'

"Let me remind you that two of my Guard, accidentally wounded when Mr. Cameron was at Tipton, are at St. Louis. Will you have them looked up? Either already at St. Louis, or somewhere between Tipton and St. Louis. Please have them cared for."

## X.

### AT SPRINGFIELD.

"Springfield, Oct. 27, 1862.

"All last night and to-day the troops were lining the road on their march from Bolivar to this place. I arrived this afternoon, and have here the Third Division, under General Sigel, together with Colonel Marshall's regiment and Major Holman with his sharpshooters. The Guards of course. All these are active officers and good troops. General Sigel with a part of his division has formed the advance of the army, and on this march has again proved himself a good and skilful officer.

"General Asboth with his division will be up to-morrow night. General Pope is next on the road, and General McKinstry will probably come in the next. We made fine marching. Yesterday Marshall's regiment of infantry made a hard march, and to-day they marched from Bolivar to Springfield, thirty miles, getting into their camp before dark. General Sigel with his whole division marched twenty miles. You will have many details of the good fight which the Guards made here, and every detail will go to show you what a brave charge it was. Three different regiments constituted the force here, under the command of Frazer and other colonels. I am pained that our loss has been so severe. As soon as I reached the town I rode to the hospital where I found fourteen of my brave Guards lying in their uniforms, side by side, in narrow, rough, plank coffins. One was brought in and laid by them while I was in the room; he was quite young, a Kentucky boy, who had been, I think, a clerk in the company. He had been taken prisoner, and was brought in, — wretchedly beaten to death with muskets, apparently, — from about seven miles out. Another died in a room above while I was in the hospital. With two exceptions our wounded will probably all recover. Charley recognized some of his particular friends among the killed, and cried and sobbed when he was telling me about it just now. On the other side eighty-three were killed, according to what can be learned here, and the wounded we cannot well know. Our officers apparently were singled out in the scattering fight through the town. Every one of them, officers and non-commissioned officers, lost from one to three horses during the fight.

Many horses had been buried before I got here, but twenty dead still remained on the field, and as I told you, we left sixty wounded twenty-five miles back. We have a good number of prisoners, some of them wounded, and some of their wounded are in and about the town.

"I wish Captain McKeever to send me up immediately all the rest of the Guards who are at St. Louis, with direction to follow me to my camp. Ask him to arm them thoroughly with sabres and revolvers; — to have them otherwise thoroughly equipped and expedited through to me.

"I send you the names of killed and wounded. Major White, who had been captured before the engagement, escaped and recaptured, and again escaped, is here with me only slightly hurt. So write to his mother."

"J. C. F."

"Springfield, Oct. 28, 1861.

" A beautiful, cool, bright morning. The funeral of our Guards will take place to-day at one o'clock. You remember that I told you in the charge some forty horses fell, and the greater part of their riders necessarily were obliged to escape into the woods, being separated from the command and unable to get hold of other horses, as some did. I am afraid that a number of them will have been butchered by the enemy who hung around the town until the reinforcements got up, which was yesterday at daybreak. I therefore may have a greater loss to tell you of, but hope not, — we don't know yet. Meantime, our men are greatly exasperated by condition of the boy brought in as I told you in my letter of yesterday, and by the hanging of a Union man and boy yesterday not far off, by the secession troops. Therefore the parties which I have thrown forward over the neighboring country will do rough work if they come upon any of the enemy. Many scenes will interest you in the fight. The war will have nothing more splendid to record. Send me up a flag for the Guard when the remainder of them come up, and have them come quick. And they may hurry up the transportation now, for if it was intended in this way to keep us from moving, the plan has failed, and we hold to-day the key of the State. The Legislature intended to meet here. First at Neosho, and then here. Part of them were here a few days ago, but we rather hurried up their travelling. After a little I shall be able to tell you what plans I may form. I am getting a little uneasy about Paducah; but General Smith is so good an officer, and the place so strong, that I think I may trust it, with what will be done by other forces. The time for the funeral has come, and I close to let Express go at once.

"J. C. F."

---

"SPRINGFIELD, Oct. 29, 1862.

"I have nothing special this morning to tell you, — that is, nothing special done yesterday, and whatever it is that is to be done, it is never safe to trust to a letter. I attended the funeral of my Guards yesterday; they were buried with military honors. The Union people begin to raise their heads since our arrival, and a procession of Union women walked by the side of the cortége to the grave. I saw big tears falling from the eyes of the men who surrounded the graves. I have not time to write you the incidents; — you must read what the reporters say. . . .

"I must not forget to say that a portion of the men unhorsed in the charge and left behind, held the town continuously until the reinforcements arrived. The fence rails are in many places riddled with balls where the action took place, and within the wood where our people charged upon the infantry, I saw yesterday four horses of the Guard lying dead within ten steps of each other, in one group. A little dog, (terrier,) " the Corporal," belonging to the Guards, charged with them, and remained on the field until twelve at night, sitting by the side of one of the wounded Guards, who was not brought in until that time. Another one of the Guards was brought in last evening from a distance of eight miles, — a prisoner and murdered, like the one I told you of in my letter of yesterday. . . . . .

"The loss of the Guards, so far as ascertained,* is fifty-two in killed, wounded, and missing — one third of the whole number. I sent out strong reconnoitring parties yesterday. At night some prisoners were brought in: a Lieutenant-Colonel Price and fourteen others. It is thought that among the force routed here was a regiment from Arkansas. The weather continues fine. . . . . .

"I notice in one of the Journals that it was upon a Report by Adjutant-General Thomas of his examination into the administration of my department that the

* The real loss was reduced to seventeen, by exchange of prisoners and recovery of wounded.

Cabinet met in council. A bitterly hostile and . . . . Adjutant-General to ride through my department and pronounce upon my conduct, without producing any authority from the President, who only was competent to order such an injurious proceeding, and without any intimation to me of such a purpose! Let them go on. . . . . . .

"J. C. F."

## XI.

#### THE DEAD.

"The land is full of farewells to the dying,
And mournings for the dead."

MAJOR CORWINE told me that when the Kentucky Company was leaving Cincinnati, the train was surrounded by their friends, — "more pretty girls than I ever saw together before — crying, but looking brave, and willing for them to go."

For these same dear ones other women shed tears, — women who, daring to look, first saw them as they charged through the streets of their home, and gave their answering prayers to the wild battle-cry for the Union; — these women followed, grateful and weeping, those who had brought back to them the protecting flag; — but now

> "Red hand in the foray
> How sound is thy slumber!"

I have been told of one of these much-tried women, who painfully and with the aid of crutches, followed in this funeral, that her husband and son had both been killed, and herself wounded, by a guerilla party. Robbed also during Price's occupation of Springfield, she was quite dependent on a son-in-law. In the fighting through the streets he was accidentally killed. And yet this woman could and did do honor by her presence to those who had deprived her of her last support. And this was the kind of people from whom all protection was withdrawn!

"CUMMINSVILLE, Nov. 2, 1861.

"DEAR SIR,—

"I received your letter of October 30, and thank you kindly for its favor. Your dispatch in the 'Gazette' of this morning moved us to tears, as did also the list of killed and wounded in the 'Enquirer,' copied from the 'St. Louis Republican.' William Vanway, one of our neighbors, is among the dead. He was one of a very fine family. His father died about a year ago, and news has just arrived of the death of his brother, in Western Virginia, in the Guthrie Gray Regiment, and right upon that is the death of William at Springfield. The mother is overwhelmed at her loss. . . . .

"Very truly your friend,
"J. F. LAKEMAN.
"To Major R. M. CORWINE,
  "A. D. C. and Judge Advocate."

When some great grief leaves one blinded and dizzy, with no power to comprehend the uprooted life or accept its new conditions, — then through the helpless, fevered mind come floating consoling words of Scripture, — verses that seemed so far off but a little while ago are now stamped vividly and forever in new meaning on our changed lives.

> "Who ne'er his bread in sorrow ate,
>    Who ne'er throughout the midnight hours
> Weeping, upon his bed has sate, —
>    He knows ye not, ye Heavenly Powers."

As in those pictures where the fewer principal figures are relieved against a groundwork of shadowy faces filled with unutterable woe, so back of our armies in the field I see that noble army of martyred women who "dwell in the shadow of the mountain." Theirs is the "dull, deep anguish of patience," — they are being trained to endure. For them the most we can do is so sadly little; but "the end shall tell."

---

"To weary hearts, to mourning homes,
　God's meekest angel gently comes;
　No power has he to banish pain,
　Or give us back our lost again;
　And yet, in tenderest love, our dear
　And Heavenly Father sends him here.

"There's quiet in that angel's glance,
　There's rest in his still countenance;
　He mocks no grief with idle cheer,
　Nor wounds with words the mourner's ear;
　But ills and woes he may not cure
　He kindly trains us to endure.

"Angel of Patience! sent to calm
Our feverish brow with cooling palm, —
To lay the storms of hope and fear,
And reconcile life's smile and tear;
And throbs of wounded pride to still,
And make our own our Father's will!

"Oh thou, who mournest on thy way!
With longings for the close of day,
He walks with thee, that angel kind,
And gently whispers, 'Be resigned, —
Bear up, bear on, the end shall tell,
That God has ordered all things well.'"

## "DEAD ON THE FIELD OF HONOR."

Those who were killed in action at Springfield, Missouri, on the 25th October, 1861, were —

### Co. A.

Corporal D. F. Chamberlain, St. Louis, Mo.
Corporal Julius Baker, St. Louis, Mo.
Wagoner F. C. Frantz, St. Louis, Mo.
Private George Dutro, St. Louis, Mo.
Private Herman Fry, St. Louis, Mo.
Private Louis Osburg, St. Louis, Mo.

### Co. B.

Corporal Francis Schneider, St. Louis, Mo.
Private Dennis Morat, St. Louis, Mo.
Private J. Nellmann, St. Louis, Mo.
Private Mitchell Rose, St. Louis, Mo.
Private G. M. Schrack, St. Louis, Mo.
Private William Wright, St. Louis, Mo.

### Co. C.

Corporal John Morrison, Indiana.
Corporal William Vanway, Cincinnati, Ohio.
Private E. Davis, Hamilton Co., Ohio.
Private Alexander C. Linfoot, Covington, Ky.

## XII.

### THE BEGINNING OF THE END.

S⒯. Paul asks, "Who goeth a warfare at any time of his own cost? or who planteth a vineyard, and eateth not of the fruit thereof?"

---

"Springfield, October 30, 1861.

"I received your note of Thursday night yesterday morning. A little postscript, added on Friday morning, tells me that the reports concerning my removal and General McClellan's victory were not confirmed. I assure you I am getting pretty well tired of being badgered in this way. I ought to have all my energies here employed against the enemy, and all the aid from Washington, moral and physical, that the government can give. In daily expectation of being removed, my subordinate officers encouraged in disobedience by the conduct of . . . . . , and the rigid rule which should govern an army moving in face of the enemy disregarded by superior officers, it becomes nearly impossible for me to calculate upon the execution of any plan. I cannot and I do not rely upon the success of any combination I may make, because I am not able to rely upon the execution of the orders I send back. In fact, I do not now venture to make any combinations. Our success to this point is due to taking just what force I could gather around me and moving right along, regardless of the rest, and trusting to our own ability to provide resources for all contingencies. But I am getting tired of this business. You can see, and it is plain to be seen, that in this way the success of the war and the interests of the country are put at great hazard. As I said to you, in the means taken to break me down, . . . . . . are certainly betraying the interests of the country. Now was the time, the accepted time, for making great progress in the war, but the days of the Republic are being numbered while the power of the government sleeps. So I am getting tired of all this, and you must not be surprised, if this goes on, to find me throwing up the reins. But I will be governed by the events of the next few days.

"General Asboth arrived with his division yesterday. Hunter is reported coming up next behind him, ( . . . . . . . . . . . . . . . . . ) Pope next, and McKinstry said to be in the rear. Notwithstanding some hard marches that I have given them, and scarcity of the usual food, the troops are in the best possible disposition. The Zagonyi charge has given tone to the army, and we see it already working. I have the satisfaction to tell you that my Delawares came in yesterday afternoon, — Fall-Leaf, who has been with me before, and fifty of his good men. They are encamped here close by me.

"All reports so far fix the enemy at Neosho up to Monday afternoon. To-day I shall probably have positive information in regard to them. I am in communication with General Price, concerning exchange of prisoners and some other points. The weather is fine to-day. Lieut. Heppner arrived, and I take him with me this morning, to select ground for General Hunter. I expect to see Howard to-morrow night, and I think he probably will bring me some definite intelligence regarding Washington. You must not think me discouraged when I say I am tired of this; but I am impatient. I feel outraged at their continued indignities, and I am always asking myself, *Cui bono?* Why do I endure it? They are sapping my character; why not at once protest against them? So don't think me discouraged. I feel well, strong, and ready for any emergency, and, above all, I feel the most unqualified contempt for . . . . And how does the nation endure it? Contending for great principles, — a vital war, — how can the people stand quietly by, and see their blood and treasure so thrown away? Squandered by demagogues in personal cabals, when the true objects of the war, taken together, are probably the grandest for which a nation ever contended in arms, — its own national existence, and the fate of one of the quarters of the world! But there is no use, now and here, to talk of this.

"Didn't we do a good thing in striking so far and so deadly a blow, and throwing the head of our column so suddenly into the key of the South? It took them all by surprise, — friends and enemies. In their retreat through the country, the enemy reported that they were attacked by 2500 men. . . . .

"I send special messenger for the Guards. Hurry up Constable's Battery, if it is in any way possible to get him; and a thousand of the Austrian altered muskets would be most acceptable, if we could have them sent at once. All, of course, if I am to remain here.

"It may show you the willingness of the German troops to do their duty, to say that General Asboth's division had nothing but meat for four days, and the General reports that they have nothing else to-day. Still they have done their duty well and cheerfully, although their health must suffer. . . . .

"J. C. F."

---

"Headquarters Western Department,
"Springfield, Oct. 30, 1861.

". . . . . . .

"Ere this, I doubt not, Adlatus Jack will have reached you, with his public budget of 'glorious news,' and his private package of items of personal adventure and experience. Nevertheless, I write you a few lines by the morning express; for

I doubt much whether the Captain's private package will find time to be opened, and I know that by the time this reaches you, he will be again at his post, and a word from his brother-in-arms will not be unacceptable.

"At the same time, you must excuse the unfamiliar look of this handwriting. Dr. Tellkampf has just performed a slight surgical operation on my right hand, and I am obliged, on account of bandages, &c., to hold my pen in an entirely new manner. I always felt, intuitively, that that man would draw my blood at the first decent opportunity, with malignant satisfaction. However, I will not scoff at him, since he has saved me from a 'felon's doom.'

"We are in Springfield, and occupying the old headquarters of General Lyon.

Sigel has his own former quarters. Asboth is encamped about half a mile from us. The other divisions have not yet arrived.

. . . . . .

"Let me turn to some pleasanter subject, — say the dust. Oh, plagues of Egypt! will you oblige me by paling your ineffectual fires? The Dust is conqueror here. I have seen my own proud chieftain bow before it, his glory obscured and hidden in its cloudy folds. Ralph and his wisp broom are as Mrs. Partington and her mop before it. Our tents are pitched in a yard, close on the street; and, as a consequence, the street comes often into camp. We see one another darkly; we feel gradually the great truth that we are but dust; we bite the dust in our humility. There is but one antidote which is here in sufficient quantity,—*Contrabands*. With five darkeys, one can keep clean just five minutes; but the operation of being brushed is wearisome after the first half hour. But, seriously, it is a very interesting sight the number of slaves who have fled to us from secession masters. One man now in my employ was waiting in the woods two months 'fur dis yer crowd to come,'—as he irreverently spoke of our army. He had been handcuffed and whipped, and ran away. His master was formerly good to him, but had treated him harshly since the loss of Springfield. One other I have,—a clear-eyed, bright quadroon boy. He and his brother are in camp, and I hope mine will turn out so well suited to me that I can take him back to the North when we return. Every one on the staff is getting rapidly supplied with his necessary article. The camp swarms with contrabands of various hues. The two brothers of whom I spoke are so white that I could not believe them slaves. The abolitionists *per se* in our midst — Colonel Lovejoy and others — find their hands full. Sable visitors come to the gallant Colonel at all hours, and are not turned away.

. . . . . . .

"Wamba appears to command my presence in the 'pavilion,' (where there is just room for two.) He winks as usual, and calls me Mr. Hayball. If I undertook to set him right, he would wink himself into an apoplexy over the sudden idea, — so I let it rest. . . .

"As for your humble servant, he has been busy enough since the departure of Captain Howard; and hopes he has not utterly failed in his attempt to supply the deficiency made by that Adlatus' absence. In addition to various other charges and duties, I am accidentally the chosen victim of the Delaware Indians, to the number of fifty-two, who bring their troubles and desires to me. Fall-Leaf commands, and Johnny-cake interprets them. Behold the bound which no Adlatus shall dare to pass, — the end, I mean, of the first four pages. This may be the last letter the 'lieutenant' writes you. I feel sure we shall see the enemy erelong, — and the enemy has promised me a captain's straps. R."

---

For the week following the twenty-fifth October, Springfield saw good days. The long subjection to the rebels was over, and the Unionists were exultant. For the first time, since early in August, they were in communication with the rest of the country. Daily mails now ran to St. Louis; an officer in uniform could travel alone by stage the whole distance, — a thing impossible when we reached St. Louis, even between the arsenal and headquarters. The General had made an agreement with General Price, by which hostilities were to be confined to the regular armies in the field, and guerrilla parties of both sides suppressed; rebels were offered protection on laying down their arms, and observing all the laws; and irresponsible arrests by any Federal soldier or official, for differences of opinion, were also prohibited. General Price had with him some ten or fourteen thousand Missourians, who did not wish to cross into Arkansas, and if they could secure protection, they were more than willing to lay down their arms, and live in peace. To keep them so would have been our affair afterward; but it was an army dispersed, and a victory gained without bloodshed, to carry out this agreement.

This agreement, so unmistakably for the best interests of Missouri, was annulled immediately upon the removal of General Frémont, when the order to reverse the engine went into effect. But, while the negotiations were going on, the General only waited for the delayed divisions to give battle.

"Headquarters Western Dept.,
"Springfield, Nov. 1, 1861.

. . . . . . . .

"But first let me say how well I found the General, — looking splendidly, in capital spirits, very glad to get news from home, very much pleased with the photographs, and 'entirely satisfied' with the 'very good time' in which my little task had been completed. Do not think that I impute my own lively emotions to the General, who is generally reserved in expression of his feelings. All of the above statements, except the splendid appearance, are from his own lips. He is only a little annoyed that the other divisions have been so slow in coming up, as he wishes to strike while he has the opportunity of a standing, not a retreating foe. But they are expected along to-day or to-morrow.

"I arrived in Springfield on Thursday morning, at ten o'clock, — three days and two hours after leaving you in St. Louis, — and should have been here the day before, had I not been obliged to bring one horse all the way through (and a borrowed one at that), and so was exercised in my mind lest he should be disabled, and fail me on the way; but he brought me through beautifully.

"I can tell you, the change from camp to St. Louis and to the road again, was something rather dazzling — or, perhaps, *dazing* — in its effects; and although I enjoyed my brief visit extremely, I feel that it must have been unsatisfactory to you, from the many things which I now remember I had to tell you. However, I console myself that it was only the gossip which was left out, — the news I gave. Just twenty-four hours after I was sitting in the 'luxurious dining-room of the Oriental palace' with you all to talk to, and a nice supper before me, I lay on the ground under a tree, talking with a rough orderly, and munching a piece of hard bread and a bit of cold meat.

. . . . . . .

"They ran, taking White with them. About twelve miles distant they, his guard, stopped at the house of a Union man, who, when he learned that White was a prisoner, went out and collected about seventeen Home Guards. Frank, hearing them outside, slipped out, and heading them, *captured his captors*, and brought them back to Springfield. Here he found Zagonyi's dead and wounded, and his two flags flying, but only a few members of the Body Guard, and some of his own men, amounting in all to twenty-six. With these men he held the town, placing out pickets all around, leaving a reserve of his sick self and one lieutenant, for twenty-four hours, till Sigel entered. He so acted as to make the enemy suppose Sigel already there; received a flag of truce from them, gave them permission to bury their dead and take their wounded, and carried the whole thing through with a bold face. H."

---

"Springfield, Nov. 1, 1861,
"10 A. M.

"The rebel Legislature passed a secession ordinance at Neosho and adjourned to Cassville. Three days since, their entire army came out of their lines at Neosho and directed their course eastward and southwardly, moving across our front and threatening us by advanced corps pushed forward on the road to Mount Vernon, and on the road from

Cassville to this place. The entire strength of Price's army is reported at 33,000. As I advised you might be the case, I am disposed to think that Pillow or Hardee's force may be moving across the country to join them. But I shall soon know, and it makes very little difference to me whether they have ten or fifteen thousand more or less when I get my little army concentrated. Hassendeubel's regiment will join us this morning. Lane and Sturgis will be in with their forces by noon. Pope will probably be in with his division by nightfall, and McKinstry with his tomorrow. I had been misinformed about General Hunter. He had been reported as being near Quincy, but his own report, which I received two days since, left him at Mount View, about fifteen miles this side of Warsaw. He had sent back a supply train for provisions, and was intending to wait for it. Yesterday at 2 A. M. I sent him a despatch, directing him to come forward. The force is rapidly getting into excellent condition, and I really think can whip the enemy two to one. I shall move with all the skill that I can bring to the work, and at the same time with as much rapidity as is consistent with it. Your letter by Captain Howard, was very pleasant to me. I am very glad to see that our movements have given so much satisfaction to our friends. . . . .

"Meantime, whatever force remains behind, hurry in. I received yesterday the despatch, which I enclose to Captain McKeever, from Governor Randall. I direct him to order the regiment immediately to St. Louis, thence to Rolla to replace Colonel Gessler's regiment, which I desire to come here to me in the field direct, the very moment it can leave Rolla. I am pleased to see that Constable's Battery has left. We want all the sabres that can come, and revolvers, and also all the altered Austrian muskets that can be spared. Hurry up the Guards, and have the requisition for their clothing filled. I think it is going to snow — it looks and feels like it. . . . .

"J. C. F."

---

"SPRINGFIELD, Nov. 2,
"9½, A. M.

. . . . .

"I now look to see the supply trains come up. In my judgment, it is absolutely certain that if we could have had them so as to have brought up the other divisions to this place concurrently with myself, we should have before this routed Price and captured his baggage-trains. I trust in you to do all that can be done. It would have been a good thing, if Major Allen had gone to Tipton to push the supplies forward. Make thanks to our friends Captain Foote and Major Corwine, and particularly to Colonel Fiala. Tell him I appreciate fully his fidelity and ability, and would have been glad, had I been able, to carry out all his able suggestions in regard to St. Louis and the Mississippi line. . . .

"The enemy's movements are still a little uncertain; — scouts, spies, and other information reported last night his advance a little nearer, but to-day will give us more positive information. Their intention is reported to occupy Wilson's Creek, and have a battle on the same ground as the other in August last. I don't believe it, and think they would have rather a merry time in carrying out their point. I am just sending out a strong reconnoitring party to make a military map of the old battle-ground and vicinity of Wilson's Creek. Hassendeubel's regiment, and Generals Sturgis and Lane got in with their forces yesterday. McKinstry with his division will be in to-day. Pope ought to reach here to-day or to-morrow. We are all right here. . . . . .

"Meantime, have Capt. McKeever send off the Fitz H. Warren Regiment to me — all of it if possible — and Colonel

Crafts Wright's regiment. Tell him, if it be not already done, to order it off instantly and peremptorily; if the order be not instantly obeyed, to place the Colonel in arrest by my order, and every other officer, if necessary. Hurry up the Guards. I suppose, if I am to remain in command, it will be settled by the time you receive this, definitely one way or the other. . . . .

"Captain —— just read me a letter, through a reliable source, which gives the contents of a despatch from Washington, dated October 28. Despatch says: 'General Scott retires from the command of the army on account of his infirmities. Orders from the Commander-in-Chief have been sent by the President to General Curtis at St. Louis, to be delivered to General Frémont, unless he is in front of the enemy, or pursues him to give him battle. The orders direct General Frémont to surrender his command to the next officer, General Hunter.' It is quite time that all this should cease. .

"Nov. 2d, 10½. — I have just received the order relieving me of my command, directing me to turn it over to General Hunter. Get quietly ready for immediate departure from St. Louis. I shall leave this place forthwith for St. Louis. . . . .
"J. C. F."

## XIII.

### THEIR RETURN.

"Return Road, near Bolivar,
"Tuesday, Nov. 5, 1861.

"So far on our return road, all is good health, good spirits, and satisfied mind. . .

"It seems to me simply a laid-out piece of work, in which I have been doing my part. . . .

"I received General Scott's order to turn over the department to Hunter, on the 2d, and the same day I had printed and published the brief General Order, transferring my command to him, and the enclosed address to the army.

"I send Raymond forward to make

the railroad arrangements, and advise you of us. We propose to embark on the cars on Thursday night, and reach St. Louis early on Friday;—the Sharpshooters, Body Guard, and a few of the Staff, together with all our horses. Further advices by telegraph. Day is breaking, and we must be on the road. Good-by — plenty of love to —— and ——, and regards to all friends.

"The order reached me when I was in face of the enemy and manœuvring with him, he being nine to twelve miles distant. Hunter came in the night, after the order of march and battle had been written, and six the next morning the hour appointed for the march against the enemy. All right. I think now there will be no battle.

"J. C. F."

The General was to have been at home by nine in the morning; but the management of the trains being in other hands, they were delayed until nearly that hour in the evening. But patient crowds had kept their watch through the long day, and by night it was a sea of heads in all the open spaces around our house. The door-posts were garlanded, and the very steps covered with flowers,—touching and graceful offerings from the Germans. China-asters and dahlias, with late roses and regular bosquets of geraniums, beautified the entrance and perfumed the air; and when the General did make his way at last through the magnificent assemblage, it was to be met by the wives and children of the German officers he had left at Springfield. Unknown to me, they had come to speak their hearts to him, but they had more tears than words. Touched to the heart already, the General was not prepared for the arrival of citizens—American as well as German—who came to thank him for past services, and ask to stand by him in the hour of disgrace. Meantime, the unceasing cheers and shouts of the vast crowd without sounded like the tide after a high wind. I could not stand it; I went far up to the top of the house, and, in the cold night air, tried to still the contending emotions, when I saw a sight that added to the throbbing of my heart. Far down the wide avenue the serried crowd was parting, its dark, restless masses glowing in the lurid, wavering torchlight, looking literally like waves;—and, passing through them, came horsemen stamped with the splendid signet of battle, their wounded horses and bullet-torn uniforms bringing cries of love and thanks from those for whom they had been battling. When they halted before the door, and the sudden ring and flash of their drawn sabres added new beauty to the picture, I think only the heart of a Haman could have failed to respond to the truth and beauty of the whole scene. Were not these men for the king to delight to honor? Who could have foreseen what was the official recognition already preparing for them?

———

Before getting the General's request for a flag for them, I had already had one made, and they came in the morning to receive it. By day their war-worn appearance was still more touching. As I looked, how I wished 'that I might utter the thoughts that arose in me;' but I could only ask Major Zagonyi to say for me how I felt the honor they had brought on our name, and that they would find I did not forget them. After he had carried them the flag, and said something, which we were too far off to hear, they returned to their camp (for the Guard was never in quarters, and lived in open camp even in St. Louis).

I give the following note as Zagonyi sent it to me: —

"I thank you, Madame, sincerely, in the name of my officers and men, for the mark of your regard in giving us this beautiful flag. Was a profound regret to them and to me that we return from the field with so short a glimpse of the rebel army.

"As we followed our leader past the

outside pickets around Springfield, our band performed their gayest music; but to me was like a funeral dirge. And it was a funeral — there were buried the fruits of three months' labor of the General, — the aspiration of thousands of ambitious men who followed his standard, — and gone, too, the hope of patriots that was ended the war in Missouri.

"But I believe in the resurrection. I believe not always will be denied truth and justice to General Frémont; will come the time — and soon — when the campaign in Missouri will be known as is in reality, well planned, well done, and how cruel and unjust it was ended.

"But is not for me to praise or criticize his action. My command did serve him when to them he could promise an honorable and active career; they will not fail from his side now that every sound of battle is banished from their ear forever."

I wish I could pass over in silence the treatment to which the Guard was now subjected; but I cannot undo facts. Only those who have experienced the infinite littlenesses of garrison tyranny can realize in how many ways they were harassed, and finally deprived of absolute necessaries.

After refusing them pay, rations, or forage, it was said they were to be put on duty as the Guard to . . . This was the drop too much, and explains the following despatch: —

(COPY OF TELEGRAM.)

"St. Louis, Missouri,
"November 11, 1861.
"Maj.-Gen. Geo. B. McClellan,
"Commanding-in-Chief,
"Washington, D. C., —

"I would regard it as an act of personal courtesy and kindness to me, if you will order my Body-Guard to remain with me, subject to no orders in this department but my own. It is composed of educated and intelligent young men, to whom the country and I owe more than the usual consideration accorded to the rank and file of the army.

(Signed) "J. C. Frémont,
"*Maj.-Gen. U. S. A.*"

(COPY.)

"By Telegraph, 11 P. M.
"HEAD-QUARTERS OF THE ARMY,
"WASHINGTON, Nov. 11, 1861.

"Major-General J. C. FRÉMONT, —

"Before receiving your despatch, I had given instructions that the cavalry corps, known as your Body-Guard, should be otherwise disposed of. Official information had reached this city that members of that body had at Springfield expressed sentiments rendering their continuance in the service of doubtful expediency. With every desire to gratify your wishes, I do not see exactly how I can violate every rule of military propriety. Please reply.

"GEO. B. MCCLELLAN,
"*Com.-in-Chief.*"

(TELEGRAM.)

"St. Louis, Nov. 12.
"Major-General Geo. B. McClellan,
"Commander-in-Chief U. S. Army, —

"I am not informed of any expression of sentiment at Springfield by the cavalry known as my Body-Guard, which should create a doubt as to the expediency of their being retained in the service of the country; while on the contrary the service rendered by the gallantry of their conduct on the 25th October at Springfield justly entitles them to the favorable consideration of the government. In view of this fact, I request the Commanding General to reconsider the case, if any severe measure has been directed against them.

"J. C. Frémont,
"*Major-General U. S. A.*"

This being unanswerable, remained unanswered.

Meantime the Guard had the additional pain of parting from the horses which had shared their hardships and triumphs; had to turn into the quartermaster's department the animals they had trained and whose wounds they had tended so carefully to make them again fit for service. General Sturgis was sent to muster them out, and whilst waiting for him, Zagonyi had them photographed as they stood in front of the rough plank-roofed shed which formed their quarters. A keen wind is blowing; the band have overcoats, but the Guard are still without; some are mounted, for the last time; more than half are on foot. General Sturgis, after reviewing them, declared he could not bring himself to think of losing such soldiers, and refused to muster them out, asking Zagonyi to wait a little until he could carry out a plan for them. His note shows the flimsiness of the pretext for disbanding them.

"St. Louis, Mo., Nov. 27, 1861.

"Major: —

"I am directed by the Major-General Commanding to muster the Body-Guard out of service; but at the same time he authorizes me to say to you that if you will raise a regiment (cavalry), retaining such officers of the Body-Guard as you may think proper, it will be accepted into the United States service.

"I am, Major,
 "Very Respectfully,
  "Your ob'd't serv't,
   "S. D. Sturgis,
    "*Brigadier-General U. S. Vols.*
"To Major Zagonyi,
 "*Commanding Body-Guard,*
  "*St. Louis, Mo.*"

Major Zagonyi declined the idea for himself, but submitted the note to the Guard. General Sturgis's generous efforts were too late. The Guard had borne as much as is right for men to bear, and they refused unanimously to accept any other organization than the one originally entered on.

From the time of the General's turning over the records, he directed the guard-mounting before the house to be discontinued. But although after some repetitions the order was obeyed, yet each night I heard the old sound of the Guard on duty inside the house, and they would not discontinue it. The day we left for New York, as we came down the steps, I saw at once that the Guard was in place at the gate, and they flashed their salute as the General passed. The countenance of one caught my attention, and after we were in the carriage both of us noticed that in returning his sabre he struck it home with his open palm as though expressing an intention not again to draw it. As he looked up, he saw that we were noticing him; and, coming down to the side of the carriage, without a word spoken, he drew off the heavy gauntlet and laid his open hand within the General's with such a blended look of dumb rage and regret and fidelity as was wonderful to see. And this was the end. On reaching New York we found this despatch, dated " St. Louis, Nov. 28th," (Thanksgiving day!)

"To Major-General FRÉMONT,
"Astor House:—
"The Body-Guard was to-day mustered out of service.      CHAS. ZAGONYI,
"*Major Com'd'g.*"

---

"But the large grief that these enfold
Is given in outline — and no more."

---

## XIV.

### PAYING GENERAL FRÉMONT'S MEN.

(Extract from the Daily Journals.)

" A bill has been prepared directing the Secretary of War to pay off all officers and men whose services were accepted and actually employed by Major-General FRÉMONT, or by the Commanding-General of Missouri, whether they were regularly mustered into service or not. It also provides that the wounded and disabled of such shall draw bounty and pensions, and the heirs of the killed draw pay and bounty as in other cases. *This bill fully provides for the Frémont Body-Guard, and relieves the government of the charge of injustice.*"

"NEW YORK,
"Dec. 17, 1861.
"HON. CHARLES B. SEDGWICK,
"Washington City,—

"I have read to-day of the bill for the payment of officers appointed by "Major-General FRÉMONT, or by the Commanding General of Missouri." I think the bill ought not to pass in its present form. To meet the many irregular appointments in that department, and in the merest ordinary justice to the officers who served their country thoroughly and well, such a bill ought to be passed, but with some modifications. Other officers in the Western Department made appointments under pressure of the same necessity that forced me to do so. I was sent to the Western Department with unrestricted authority, which comprehended the power to appoint, but I judged it safer to make the application which gave me that authority, direct, ample, and explicit, from the Secretary at War and the President. The bill ought to recognize the fact that the irregularity — if there was any which could render these appointments less legal than any others made by the government — is justly chargeable upon government, and not upon myself acting under its direction.

"As it now stands the bill carries the idea that the interposition of Congress is required to prevent my officers from suffering by my unauthorized acts. Suffering, they undoubtedly are.

"This bill claims further to do away with any injustice to the Body-Guard by paying them. Their pay is their right, not a favor. They were regularly enlisted with the usual forms. They rendered good and valuable service from the day of their enlistment. They performed one of the most gallant acts ever recorded in this or any other war. My letter on their behalf was not replied to. On the contrary, on their return to St. Louis — just after their victory — they were treated with marked disrespect by the government officials; refused forage for their horses, rations for themselves, pay or clothing. Instead of commendation for merit they were met by an order directing them to be disbanded, and 'not to be retained in the service of the country, for certain sentiments alleged to have been expressed by them at Springfield.' This is the injustice of which the Guard and their friends complain. It is not a question of money, and this bill does not remove the charge.

"For the present I merely wish to call

your attention to this point. Perhaps an opportunity will be found to have their services recognized hereafter.

"In regard to the other point of the bill, I have to ask that you will endeavor to have such amendment made as will suit the view I have suggested.

"It is material to me to have the facts of my administration set out distinctly and fully from the authentic records. This is my first desire. But until I can reach this justice, I desire carefully to guard against any legislative action which it might be difficult to explain afterwards, as such is usually held conclusive.

(Signed) "J. C. FRÉMONT,
"&c., &c."

But what could justify (granting the pretext against those at Springfield) the dismissal of the company who had never left St. Louis, and who were guiltless of victory or " sentiments "? The regulations require that all charges shall go through the officer immediately commanding, — naturally enough, if a fair hearing and justice are to be secured. But except the vague anonymous say-so repeated by General McClellan in his despatch, no explanation has ever been made.

## XV.

> "Whate'er success awaits my future life,
> The *beautiful* is gone — *that* comes no more."

AND this is the story of the Body-Guard. It is not claimed for them that they showed a rarer courage than tens of thousands of others in this war. But theirs was the singular fortune to go to their first battle under a cloud of reproach, though blameless, and to return from it victorious, to the punishment reserved for the gravest military offences. They did their whole duty and more. They lit up the dark war-cloud, further blackened by Ball's Bluff, with a lightning ray of victory, an earnest of what was to follow. For this they were dismissed the service; the morning freshness of their love of country blighted, and its first offering rejected. It is such a grievous sin to throw back generous feelings and make trust impossible. I dreaded its effect on them. But they are proving that deeper than any self-love lies love of country. Nearly all are again in service. They have deserved higher regard than any ordinary victory can earn,—for they have conquered themselves.

When there is such a weight of sacrifice and suffering, I trust much apology is not needed for my attempt to lessen its burden on those to whose assistance this little offering is dedicated.

I think only the wife of a man much before the public can fully value the sacredness of home, and make it almost a religion to guard against any profanation of its sweet security. Born to and educated in this feeling in my father's house, and confirmed in it by the experience of my own home, it has been a real sacrifice for me to lay open even so small a part of my life. This is unnecessary to say to those who know me, but as such a vast many more do not, and, only seeing what's done, know not what's resisted, I beg of them to bear this in mind, and not think this attempt to relieve suffering more unwomanly or less needed than any of the other new positions in which women are finding themselves during this strange phase of our national life.

The restraints of ordinary times do not apply now. How many women — many of them rich in the good gifts of youth and beauty, and charm of mind — minister daily at the bedsides of men whose very names are unknown to them, overcoming, not only their shuddering repugnance to ghastly sights, but the deeper instinct of shyness and reserve. They can well bear the sneers of those whose Decameronish instinct leads them to sit apart in pleasant places, and cultivate forgetfulness while the angel of death is leaving no house unvisited. They have "waked to a higher aim:" — they "have felt with their native land and are one with their kind."

LIST OF THOSE WOUNDED IN ACTION AT SPRINGFIELD, OCTOBER 25th, 1861.

### Co. A.

| | |
|---|---|
| Sergeant Jos. C. Frock, | De Witt, Missouri. |
| Corporal Philip F. Davis, | Belleville, Illinois. |
| Corporal Edward H. Deane, | St. Louis, Missouri. |
| Private C. H. Bowman, | St. Louis, Missouri. |
| Private Frederick Lenderking, | St. Louis, Missouri. |
| Private A. J. Wisa, | St. Louis, Missouri. |

### Co. B.

| | |
|---|---|
| 1st Lieut. W. Westerborg, | St. Louis, Missouri. |
| 1st Lieut. Louis Vansteenkiste, | St. Louis, Missouri. |
| Corporal J. T. Underwood, | St. Louis, Missouri. |
| Corporal G. W. Holbrook, | St. Louis, Missouri. |
| Corporal Louis Winel, | Columbia, Illinois. |
| Private John Frank, | St. Louis, Missouri. |

### Co. C.

| | |
|---|---|
| 1st Lieut. Jos. M. Kennedy, | Covington, Kentucky. |
| 2d Lieut. James Goff, | Carbondale, Pennsylvania. |
| Sergeant Charles H. Hunter, | Hamilton Co., Ohio. |
| Private Henry M. Diggins, | Cincinnati, Ohio. |
| Private William C. Williams, | Cincinnati, Ohio. |
| Private Daniel G. Jones, | Cincinnati, Ohio. |

Private Benjamin T. Haebler, Clermont Co., Ohio.
Private Allen Purdy, Covington, Kentucky.
Private C. W. Moore, Broome Co., Ohio.
Private P. M. Murphy, Canada.
Private William Haskell, Cincinnati, Ohio.
Private Robert Lee, Cincinnati, Ohio.
Private J. R. Day, Hamilton Co., Ohio.

Two of the Prairie Scouts, whose names I have at present no means of ascertaining, were killed in the charge, and buried with the dead of the Guard.

The Prairie Scouts are still in service, and entitled to all the rewards which the country gives to its soldiers; what they did on the field is already chronicled, and their young commander is winning continued distinction in the West. But the Guard, having been dismissed the service, can receive no pension; and for them there is no other reward than the consciousness of duty well done. I have fallen far short of my hope to do them justice,—giving up the attempt to individualize, as I found the truth of Zagonyi's words, "that all was worthy of mention."

THE END.

# TROOPER'S DEATH.

Words and Music translated and arranged from the German.

## TROOPER'S DEATH. Concluded.

2 Thou springing grass, that art so green,
Shall soon be rosy red, I ween,
My blood the hue supplying!
I drink the first glass, sword in hand,
To him who for the Fatherland
    Lies dying!

3 Now quickly comes the second draught,
And that shall be to freedom quaffed
While freedom's foes are flying!
The rest, O Land! our hope and faith!
We'd drink to thee with latest breath,
    Though dying!

4 My darling! — ah, the glass is out!
The bullets ring, the riders shout —
No time for wine or sighing!
There! bring my love the shivered glass,
Charge! on the foe! no joys surpass
    Such dying!

www.ingramcontent.com/pod-product-compliance
Lightning Source LLC
Chambersburg PA
CBHW021838230426
43669CB00008B/1012